FERGUS

A Scottish Town by Birthright

Grand River, Fergus.

Grand River postcard. (Publisher's private collection, postmarked Nov. 12, 1906)

FERGUS

A Scottish Town by Birthright

PAT MATTAINI MESTERN

FOREWORD BY ARTHUR BLACK

NATURAL HERITAGE / NATURAL HISTORY INC.

Dedicated to Richard Birch, a dear friend of the family, who died in 1994 just months before realizing his dream of once again visiting his homeland, India.

On the sweet west wind you now can fly,
no longer bound as a mortal to earth;
So touch our cheek as you pass by,
to remind us again of your birth;
As a spirit now free to roam,
Those wonderful places you once called home.

Fergus: A Scottish Town by Birthright
by Pat Mattaini Mestern

Published by Natural Heritage / Natural History Inc.
P.O. Box 95, Station "O", Toronto, Ontario M4A 2M8

Design and typesetting: Robin Brass Studio
Printed and bound in Canada by Hignell Printing Limited,
Winnipeg, Manitoba

Canadian Cataloguing in Publication Data
Mestern, Pat Mattaini
Fergus : a Scottish town by birthright
Includes bibliographic references and index.
ISBN 0-920474-97-7
1. Fergus (Ont.) – History. 2. Fergus (Ont.) – Biography. I. Title.
FC3099.P47M47 1995   971.3'42   C95-931089-4
F1059.5.F47M47 1995

FRONT COVER: Fergus, view of the Grand River from dam to St. David Street Bridge c.1988, courtesy of Marjorie R. Dew, Fergus, Ontario.

BACK COVER: Fergus Main Street, looking west in the 1930s.

Natural Heritage / Natural History Inc. gratefully acknowledges the assistance of the Canada Council, the Ontario Arts Council, and the Government of Ontario through the Ministry of Citizenship, Tourism and Recreation.

Contents

Unless otherwise credited all photos are from the author's private collection or courtesy of Ted Mestern, Heather & Hearth.

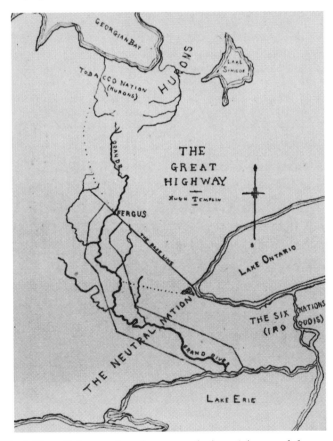

Hugh Templin's map, based on an early (c.1760) map of the area.

Foreword

My name is Black, but you can colour me green today. I'm jealous.
Of Pat Mestern.

Pat Mestern has accomplished what all writers dream of pulling off: she's made something come alive.

In this case, it is my home town – the southwestern Ontario town of Fergus, which sits on the banks of the Grand River about 60 miles off the port side of Toronto.

In this book, Ms. Mestern tracks the life of the town from pioneer days of the early 19th century which saw Indian encampments on the outskirts and bears in the schoolyard – to modern times at the end of the 20th century which sees a town with a hospital, a high school, an industrial base and more than 8,000 permanent residents.

This is history with a human face. The book is occasionally naughty, always fascinating, and – my dour old history teacher at Fergus District High School must be grimacing in his grave – frequently hilarious.

Enjoy!

Arthur Black

Arthur Black,
Writer and Broadcaster

Early Fergus. Painting by Miss J. Fordyce. Buildings from left to right include mill, distillery, pig pen, granary, Webster's Stores, Baker Walker's house, log school and first church. (Metropolitan Toronto Reference Library, John Ross Robertson Collection)

THE SETTLEMENT SITE HAS BEEN FOUND!

'Our hosts volunteered to ride with us after breakfast up the banks of the river, to view the object of our visit, distant about seven miles. The day was fine, and the prodigious height of the maples, the walnuts, elms etc., gave a solumn character to the stillness of the forest. The only trace of a road consisted in "blazes" or chips taken from the bark of the trees. Occasionally some immense overthrown trunk blocked up the only passage, and we had nothing for it then but a sporting leap a performance which the Canadian pony took his own mode of executing, somewhat to the discomposure of his rider, as it more nearly resembled the feats of grimalkin than any equestrian movement we had ever seen. The soil we found to be of first rate quality, a deep black loam, rather inclineng (sic) to sand, upon a stratum of limestone and the luxuriance of clover and other grasses was quite refreshing to look on.'

Adam Fergusson's Journal, *October 8th, 1833,*
Nichol Township, Wellington County, Upper Canada.

An Overview of Fergus

Fergus is a Scottish town by birthright, its founders, Adam Fergusson and James Webster having emigrated from the lowlands of Scotland. Both were Advocates by profession. The earliest settlers were all from Scotland with a high percentage being hand-picked by the founders. In fact many were relatives of Fergusson and Webster. Originally known as Little Falls, the fledgling settlement's name would be changed to honour Fergusson and recognize the Scottish influence. Several letters exist to suggest that the name was chosen to commemorate Fergus, Scotland's first monarch.[1] To strengthen the cultural ties, streets were named to recognize locations in Scotland, a tradition maintained to this day.

For Fergusson and Webster, the welfare of Scottish emigrants coming to Upper Canada was a primary concern. Both felt people were leaving their homeland for Canada with no knowledge of the new land. Worse yet, they had a strong suspicion these unsuspecting emigrants were being taken advantage of by unscrupulous countrymen. As Fergusson had visited Upper Canada in 1831 to look for land possibilities, he subsequently wrote a handbook for emigrants which described the lands, had lists of equipment requirements and gave costs for items.[2] He did forget, however, when publishing his handbook that many of the settlers taking advantage of promises for land in Upper Canada could not read.

In 1833 Webster and the Fergusson family emigrated. They broadened their search for suitable lands to include the southwestern regions of Upper Canada and the frontier areas to the north of Guelph. In October 1833 they visited Little Falls in Nichol Township and were impressed with what they saw. There was an abundance of trees for housing and firewood, stone for building, water for power and rich loam for cropping.

Trained as an advocate in Edinburgh, James Webster devoted much of his first twenty years in Upper Canada to the advancement of Fergus. He was Registrar of the County of Wellington until his death on February 6, 1869.

Fergusson and Webster quickly purchased approximately 7,400 acres. In December of 1833 a log cabin was raised beside a stream (behind 173 St. Andrew Street West). This first building was occupied by Webster and William Buist, an elderly gentleman affectionately known as "The Provost". It is believed members of the Black Pierpoint Settlement, which was located one quarter mile from the site, assisted with the raising of this cabin.[3]

The hardships endured by the people during the settlement's first years were typical of those faced by all early settlers, cold weather, crop failure and lack of knowledge of both farming and the area. Fergusson and Webster softened these hardships with massive injections of money for the construction of buildings, including a church, a school, mills and a store. During one particular winter, Webster gave so freely of his money

The Honourable Adam Fergusson. Noted for his agricultural interests, he was involved with early veterinary medicine, Shorthorn cattle and the beginning of the Agricultural Association of Upper Canada in 1846. Below is his wife Jemima Blair Fergusson in 1812. (H. Black)

that settlers might purchase flour, a petition was begun to change the name of the community to Websterville.[4]

Until 1850 an unwritten policy of restricted growth was implemented. Because Fergusson, Webster and other monied Scotsmen owned the lands, only Scots were allowed to purchase village lots. Webster founded the town of Arthur, a few miles north of Fergus in 1840, to accommodate those Irish people wishing to stay in the area. However, Irishmen employed by the mills in Fergus could rent homes owned by the Scots. A dispute in 1850 between Webster and Fergusson resulted in Webster moving to Guelph and selling a high percentage of his land holdings in Fergus to the Irish. Fergusson himself never did live in the community he co-founded, preferring "Woodhill", his estate on the escarpment near Waterdown.

Fergus is an attractive, quiet community of tree-lined streets with many stone homes, churches, modern schools and attractive parklands. The town is laid out on a rectangular grid with the Grand River flowing through the centre of the main heritage area. It was in the river valley that the original settlement began. Limestone riverbanks slope gently upward to level plains on the north and south of the community. In par-

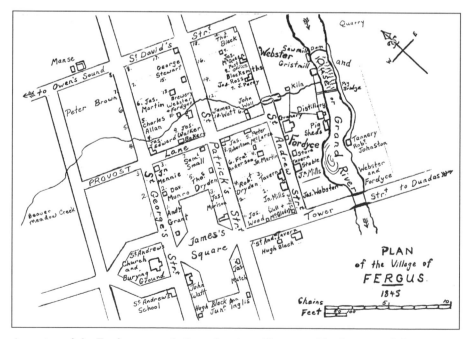

A tracing of the Fordyce map of 1845, showing villagers and landowners of that time.

ticular, the rock gorge and waterfalls created by the river, including Mirror Basin and the Whirlpool found in the centre of town, are beautiful natural resources and an attraction for visitors and townspeople alike.

A pioneer memorial, constructed of stones and other architectural items from early buildings, was dedicated in Union Square (at the junction of Tower, Union and Bridge Streets) in 1933. This interesting memorial holds the chimney from "Woodhill", the Waterdown home of Adam Fergusson, the keystone from the first mill, stones from an early tavern and from the village home of James Webster.

In 1928 and again in 1949 a village planning scheme was paid for and implemented by the village fathers at the insistence of the Beatty family.[5] Over the years the family had built a considerable fortune and with it the influence to direct the development of the community. Plans which placed an emphasis on controlled growth and attractive buildings were followed by the town fathers until the mid-1950's when the Beatty's influence over the community declined. Despite the plan's positive features, a major flaw was the lack of provision for another large industry to be built on village land. This oversight hampered the industrial growth which Fergus needed to encourage its young people to remain in the community.

People from the Past

The last of the original settlers, Mrs. James Skeoch died September 9, 1925 in her 95th year. (A.E. Byerly)

Fergus has its share of interesting individuals who contributed to its history. As was the case in many Ontario communities, eccentrics were tolerated to a greater extent then than they are today. Of course, not all of the following were eccentric, but all made invaluable additions to the fabric and character of Fergus.

Alexander Davidson was born near Fergus 1838. He took up his trade of shoe making at the age of 12 and retired 78 years later. (A.E. Byerly)

Richard (Captain Dick) Pierpoint[6]

Richard Pierpoint, Parepoint, Paupine or Pawpine (depending on who spelled the name) was a Black from Bondau, (Bondu, Boundou, again depending on which early map one reads) Senegal, Africa. Captured into slavery at age sixteen, Pierpoint spent the next eighteen years of his life as a slave in New York State. He was granted his freedom at the age of thirty-four as reward for fighting with the British during the War of Independence. He is registered as a "pioneer" in the ranks of Butlers Rangers and it was thought that he served most of his time at Fort Niagara. His name is on a list drawn up on July 20, 1784 as a disbanded Ranger intending to settle in the Niagara peninsula. He was granted two-hundred acres of land on the Twelve Mile Creek (now in St. Catharines) under his more common name of Black Dick.

In 1790 Pierpoint was one of nineteen freed Blacks to petition the Lieutenant-General of Upper Canada, John Graves Simcoe (he became Upper Canada's Lieutenant-Governor in 1791), for a Black reserve (similar to the land grant given to Joseph Brant's Native Americans). It is commonly believed that Pierpoint wrote the following petition:

> The Petition of the Free Negros.
>
> That there are a number of Negroes in this part of the County many of whom have been soldiers during the late war between Great Britian and America, and others who were born free with a few who have come, into Canada since the peace, – your Petitioners are desirous of settling adjacent to each other in order that they may be enabled to give assistance (in work) to those amongst them who may most want it,
>
> Your Petitioners therefore humbly Pray that their situation may be taken into consideration, and if your Excellency should see fit to allow them a Tract of Country to settle on, separate from the white settlers, your Petitioners hope their behaviour will be such as to show, that negroes are capable of being industrious, and that in loyalty to the Crown they are not deficient.
>
> And your memorialist Will as in
>
> – signed by 19: Robert Franklin, John Gerof, Peter Bong, Jack Baker, Richard Pierpoint, Pampadour, Jack Becker, John Cesar, John Jackson, Tom Forcy, Jack Mumwood, John Smith, Peter Green, Michael Grot, Adern Lewis, John Dimon, Simon Speek, Thomas Walker, Saisor Sepyed.
>
> Petition of 29 June 1794. Rejected read in Council July 8, 1794.[7]

It appears that the request was turned down because Simcoe felt that the early Black settlers would eventually assimilate into the white community.

Pierpoint and his friends must have felt the effects of discrimination because by 1806 he sold most of his holdings near Twelve Mile Creek, but listing himself as a farmer, he lived with other Blacks in one area of Grantham, Lincoln County. Reforms initiated by Lieutenant Governor Peter Hunter, who was purported of having no liking for Blacks, saw the suspension of Pierpoint from the United Empire Loyalist's list. Pierpoint does not appear to have appealed this suspension although he had been identified as one of the first ten United Empire Loyalists in Niagara. At some point in his life he moved from Grantham to Niagara on the Lake, then Newark.

Because of his involvement in the War of 1812-14, he and his friends were entitled to more acreage. A General Order In Council dated 19 Jan. 1820 respecting militia grants in Garafraxa in Haldimand County stipulated:

> No. 1037 (Militia) Grant to Richard Pierpoint of the Township of Grantham in the County of Lincoln in the Niagara District Farmer-as a private in the Colored Corps under Captain Runchey and Lieutenant Robertson – the Easterly half of Lot no 6 in the 1st Con: of the Township of Garafraxa – Containing one hundred acres.[8]

Although his loyalties were with the monarchy and Upper Canada, in reality his heart belonged to Africa. In 1821, only one year before accepting and moving to land in the Fergus area, Pierpoint had been petitioning the government for monies to send himself and other freed Blacks back to Africa. His petition was filed in York on July 18, 1821:

> The Petition of Richard Pierpoint, now of the Town of Niagara, a Man of Color, a native of Africa and an Inhabitant of this Province since the year 1780,
>
> Most humbly Sheweth,
>
> That Your Excellency's Petitioner is a native of Bondon (Bondore; Bondou) (sic) in Africa; that at the age of sixteen Years he was made a Prisoner and Sold as a Slave; that he was conveyed to America about the year 1760, and sold to a British officer; that he served his Majesty during the American Revolutionary War in the Corps called Butler's Rangers; and again during the late American War in a Corps of Color raised on the Niagara Frontier. That your Excellency's Petitioner is now old and without property that he finds it difficult to obtain a liveliehood by his labor; that he is above all things desirous to return to his native country; that His Majesty's Government be graciously pleased to grant him any relief; he wishes if may be affording him the means to proceed to England and from hence to a Set-

tlement near the Gambia or Senegal Rivers, from whence he could return to Bondou.

Your Excellency's Petitioner therefore humbly prays that Your Excellency will be graciously pleased to take his case into your favorable consideration and order such steps to be taken to have him sent as to Your Excellency may seem do; or to afford him relief in any manner Your Excellency may be graciously pleased to order.[9]

Adjutant General's office, York, 21 July 1821
I do hereby certify that Richard Pierpoint, a man of color, served His Majesty in North America, during the American Revolutionary War in the Provincial Corps Called Butler's Rangers.

I further Certify that the Said Richard Pierpoint, better known by the name of Captain Dick, was the first colored man who proposed to raise a Corps of Men of Color on the Niagara Frontier, in the last American War; that he Served in the said corps during the War, and that he is a faithful and deserving old Negro.[10]

Pierpoint's request for monies to return to Africa was turned down. It is also possible that the land given in 1820 was questioned because a deposition was made to ensure that he was entitled to the lands in Garafraxa .

Certificate of N. Coffin to Thomas Ridout. I hereby certify that I have carefully examined the claims of Richard Pierpoint, (a Man of Colour) of the Township of Grantham in the Niagara District, Farmer, and find him entitled to ... bounty of a Grant of the vast lands of the Crown, having served as a Private in the Colored Corps under Captain Runchey and Lieut. Robertson from the lst of September 1812, to the 24th of March 1815.

York 8 May 1821[11]

Pierpoint's fate was to remain in Garafraxa. He and his friends settled into the challenge of developing a Black "reserve" in what is known today as West Garafraxa township, located just east of Fergus.

Location ticket (duplicate) grant on fulfilment of settling dutes (sic) as req'd by Order in council of 20 Oct. 1818; to clear and fence 5 acres for every 100 acres granted; to erect a dwelling house of 16' x 20' and to clear one half of the Road in front of each lot. The whole to be performed within two years from the date of the ticket.

Date of location ticket 30 July 1822.

Note the Settlement duty performed as attested and admitted 15 Sept. 1826.[12]

This log cabin, c.1920, was one of the last remaining log cabins in the Pierpoint settlement. Old Harriett, right, was one of the last surviving members of her Pierpoint Settlement family. (A.E. Byerly)

Their community, which emcompassed about half a mile square, was formed some ten years before the land for present day Fergus was purchased. In fact, Pierpoint may have given Fergus its original name of Little Falls for there was a substantial natural waterfall just down river from his land holdings. These falls were located right in the heart of what was to be the future Fergusson/Webster settlement.

Pierpoint drafted his will on January 28, 1838. As he had no heirs nor relations, his farm (in Garafraxa) was left to Lemuel Brown, a resident of Halton Township. Pierpoint definitely did not belong in Fergusson's model community, but he and Webster had developed a close relationship which lasted until Pierpoint's death in 1838, at eighty-eight years of age. Webster had wished Pierpoint to be buried in the Auld Kirkyard, but received little support from his fellow settlers. Memoirs document that a heated argument took place with members of the church stating that Pierpoint could be buried in the paupers section of the graveyard, but that no tombstone could be erected.[13]

To this day no one knows the exact place where Pierpoint is buried. It is unlikely that he would have been buried in the cemetery as it is suggested that Pierpoint himself would not have wished this. It is possible that his grave could be in Garafraxa Township on Black settlement land, or in Niagara-on-the-Lake in the Black cemetery, or perhaps in St.

Catharines. However, several people who had ancestors in the Pierpoint settlement state emphatically that Pierpoint is buried in Garafraxa Township.

During his later years, Pierpoint appears to have put a great deal of emphasis on his African heritage. He became the Groit (verbal history keeper) of the various Black communities and settlements to the north and west of Fergus. He travelled throughout the country to isolated Black areas to give encouragement and to collect family histories. His assistant, known as "Deaf Moses", became the Groit after Pierpoint's death, but was unable to maintain the tradition. As Pierpoint had, Deaf Moses also served at Queenston Heights and had suffered severe hearing loss as a result of being stationed too close to a cannon. (Since the role of a Groit is to maintain the verbal history of the community and to ensure its pass-ing on to the next generation, his unfortunate hearing loss became a liability to the role.)

Proper credit has never been given to the man known as Captain Dick, Richard Pierpoint, or Black Dick. He was one of the first ten United Empire Loyalists to come to Niagara. He fought valiantly in two wars on the side of the British (being given the name "Captain Dick" by his peers), and he was the main spokesperson for Blacks in Upper Canada. He also is recognized as an early resident of the Town of Fergus since his land stood on what is today an extension of St. Andrew Street, although not yet officially annexed to the town.

William Buist

Affectionately known as "The Provost", William Buist had a penchant for wearing a kilmarnock[14] to bed. He was an older gentleman who ar-rived in the settlement in November of 1833 and shared the first house built there with Webster. When the mill commenced operation in 1835, the first wheat to be ground under the mill's stones was from his garden.

Buist was a man who attributed his bachelorhood to the fact women thought he gave them too much freedom. He had the highest regard for women, believing they were equal to, if not better than men, and he thought women should have the legal right to vote. In 1842 when an election was held to choose an area representative to District Council, Buist was put in charge of one of the largest voting booths. He let all women who owned land enter a vote. At the time Webster, up against a man by the name of Durand, won by a slim majority. A recount revealed that "Women had voted"! Shame! Although Buist was ordered to remove all ballots cast by women, Webster still won. Undaunted, Buist continued to lobby for a legal vote for women until his death in Scotland on July lst, 1853.[15] It seems appropriate that this forward-looking gentleman should have died on the date which was later chosen as Canada's birthday. Provost Lane is named to honour this old and venerable early citizen of Fergus.

Alexander Dingwall Fordyce Jr.

Fordyce Junior, a cousin of Webster's, came to the settlement in 1835 to scout out suitable land holdings for his father and family. Alexander Fordyce Senior had committed some financial indiscretion in Scotland and had thought it prudent to "leave town". A learned man, Fordyce Jr. kept a detailed diary and sketched accurate records of the settlement as it developed. In 1839 Fordyce Jr. and his sister Elizabeth began a lending library in their home. These siblings were deeply religious and attended the Presbyterian Church. Elizabeth

A.D. Fordyce. (Wellington County Museum and Archives)

Fordyce sketch of Fergus, July 1835. Left to right: Hugh Black's tavern, Thos Young's store, school, home of Chas Allan, the cleihum (home of Webster and Buist), St. Andrews Presbyterian Church, several other dwellings, Walker's Bakery.

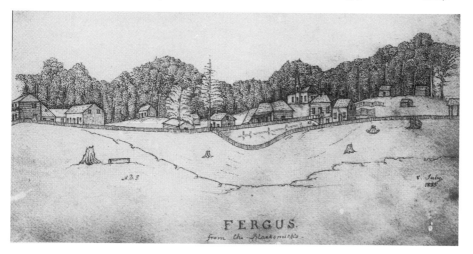

FERGUS.
from the Blacksmith's.

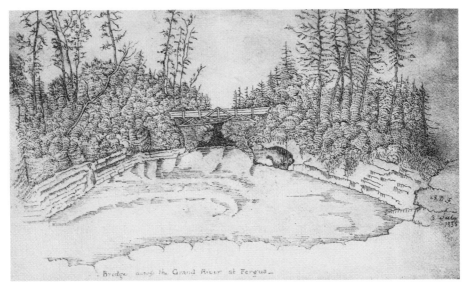

"Falls of the Grand River at Fergus" by A.D. Fordyce Jr., dated July 6, 1835.

Early sketch by A.D. Fordyce: St. Andrew Street, looking east from Tower Street.

never married, but dedicated her life to her brother and church. She was so devoted that after her death some people swore they saw her sitting in the church gallery, right hand side, front row. To this day, some declare that she is still there!

The Fordyce library consisted of books donated by the Webster,

Fergusson, Ferrier and Fordyce families. Most were scholarly works of an agricultural or religious nature. Sketches of naked Africans were torn from travel books lest the mind of the viewer be corrupted. Any reference to the Fordyce scandal in Scotland was removed from the 1790-1820's bound editions of *The Scotsman*.[16] Books from the early Fordyce library survive with Elizabeth's hand of censorship on them.[17]

Reverend Patrick Bell

The Reverend Patrick Bell. (Wellington County Museum and Archives)

An inventive man, Reverend Patrick Bell created the horse-pushed reaping machine in Scotland in 1827, but unfortunately had failed to patent it. Some years later, Cyrus McCormack of Staunton, Virginia would take full credit for the invention.

Reverend Bell arrived in Canada in 1833 with Webster and the Fergusson family to be the tutor to Fergusson's six sons at Woodhill for a stipulated period from 1833 to 1837. Whenever possible he journeyed to Fergus to spend time with Webster, a man of his own age. He did not like Canada or "Canadians" and made this quite clear in the journals he kept.[18] His disdain for Canadian farmers was only superseded by his total hatred for Americans. When he returned to Scotland in 1837, his departure was not mourned. He left with James Webster who had estate business to attend to in Scotland, but when Webster came back to Canada, Bell remained behind. Eventually he would obtain recognition for his invention.

As distasteful as he found Canadians, his journals are a marvellous record of life in Upper Canada during the 1830's. His daily weather records provide pertinent insights into the struggles of the time. Several interesting, however possibly biased, examples of his observations could change the interpretative programmes at historic sites. He wrote that many small communities had a communal outdoor bakeoven, similar to those found in Quebec; that most of the households in 1833-37 did not cook over the open fire, but had stoves; that American women were ugly, but their clothing was exceptionally attractive. On the other hand Canadian women were pretty, but their clothes were rags. He wrongly thought that the source of the Grand River was in an extinct volcano

Bell's Reaping Machine, from an old steel engraving in "Fergus, The Story of a Little Town", by Hugh Templin.

somewhere north of Little Falls. A map exists which shows the source of the Grand labelled with the word volcano.[19] He mentioned that wild game was not as plentiful as settlers were led to believe, especially in the more advanced areas of Upper Canada. He detested the fact that he was treated as a lowly tutor who had to agree with every opinion that his employer or wife might have. By the same token he spoke eloquently from the pulpit and played the flute admirably...even on occasion in the staid Presbyterian church!

George Clephane

Clephane travelled on the "Souter Johnny", the same ship which carried Mary Barker and her siblings to Canada. Mary was betrothed to Thomas Young who was the first store-keeper and postmaster in Fergus. During the voyage across the Atlantic, Clephane, a remittance man[20] became smitten with her sister Louise, a sweet maiden fifteen years old. Instead of ending his travels in Belleville where he had relatives, he followed Louise to Fergus. Settling into a comfortable life of drinking and riding fine

George Clephane's grave adjacent to St. Andrews Church receives many visits. His sister, Elizabeth, immortalized her brother (The Lost Sheep) in her popular hymn "There Were Ninety and Nine".

horses, he wooed Louise with great fervour, but knowing his vices she spurned his attentions. Ten years later Clephane was still wooing and Louise still spurning his advances.

Clephane, with his blonde hair and his height of over six feet, was a handsome fellow. An early settler, Mrs. James Skeoch, described Clephane as a fine gentleman with a generous nature. In the early 1850's Clephane met his untimely death when he fell from his horse on St. Andrew Street (in front of what is now the library building) and struck his head on a stone culvert. After his death Clephane's sister who lived in England, wrote a poem about her brother entitled, "There Were Ninety and Nine".

> There were ninety and nine that safely lay
> In the shelter of the fold.
> But one was out on the hills away,
> Far off from the gates of gold,
> Away on the mountains wild and bare,
> Away from the tender shepherd's care.[21]

The words were brought to the attention of Ira Sankey, a famous evangelist, who composed suitable music for the poem and had it sung at one of his services. Soon it became a very popular Victorian hymn. A gravestone in the Auld Kirkyard commemorates both Clephane and the hymn.

After Clephane's death Louise moved to Toronto to live with her sister, Mrs. James Lamond Smith. She never married. One must believe that she loved Clephane in view of the fact she devoted her life to helping people overcome their drinking problems. In the harbour area of Toronto, she became known as the "Saint Lady" while she went from one hotel to another, handing out temperance literature. Louise was also known for the exquisite needlework she executed on wedding gowns, church vestments and alter cloths.[22]

Doctor Abraham Groves

Abraham Groves was a late addition to Fergus, arriving with the Irish emigration surge of the 1860's. He attended high school in Fergus and medical school in Toronto. After his graduation, he returned to Fergus and set up practice in his hometown. Controversy immediately began as the brash young doctor had some unusual methods for treatment. He is best known as the first doctor to perform an appendectomy in North

America, the first doctor to boil operating gloves (his riding gloves) and the first North American doctor to give a blood transfusion.[23] His treatments were so radical that his fellow doctors tried to have him drummed out of the medical profession, citing lunacy as one reason. But Groves' patients lived and his fame spread.

An inventive man, willing to invest locally, Groves established an electric light plant in Fergus in the old tannery on the edge of the river, near the St. David bridge. By September 18, 1884 nine electric lamps were lighting St. Andrew Street. Groves gradually expanded his electrical services to include the County Poor House and the main street of Elora.

He built his own hospital, the Royal Alexandra, which was given over to the village in the 1920's. Groves served on the Village Council, owned one of the first cars in the area, kept an alligator named Adolphus (after noted local historian, Adolphus E. Byerly) and had a parrot named Polly. As well he was an accomplished poet and writer.

In his 80th year he performed eye surgery on a woman, after writing to a publishing house citing failing sight as the reason he wished to cancel his subscription to a

Left: Dr. Abraham Groves. (Wellington County Museum and Archives)

Below: The Royal Alexandra Hospital.

medical journal! Fergusites knew him as "The Beloved Physician", an inscription which appears on his gravestone. Groves was either greatly loved or thoroughly hated, and he preferred it that way. He thought it wise to know where his enemies were. One of his greatest satisfactions in life was that he outlived most of them. On May 12th, 1935, Dr. Groves died peacefully at Grovehurst, 180 Queen Street East.

After the death of Dr. Groves' second wife, Polly came under the care of Archie Anderson. The parrot lived on to be about forty-five years of age and died around 1977. Towards the end, the bird was a most horrible, scrawny looking thing, but eventually Polly was donated to the museum by Mr. and Mrs. Dickie from Fergus who were taking care of Archie's estate. They had kept the bird in their freezer for a year or so before they had it stuffed!

Polly is now on display at the Wellington County Museum, the former site of the County House of Industry and Refuge (the Poor House). Dr. Groves had been the physician at the Poor House for over fifty years and much of his knowledge about the "internal workings" of the human body was garnered from examinations of cadavers at the House. Part of his responsibilities was to identify the cause of death for the County House's records. As a result, many people owed their lives to the knowledge Dr. Groves gained by performing autopsies on the poor.

Alexander and Matilda Harvey – The Laird and Belle of Kinnettles
Alexander Harvey came to Fergus as a lad of seventeen years, in the company of James Webster when Webster returned from escorting Patrick Bell back to Scotland. In 1839, then a married man of nineteen, Harvey returned to Scotland with his bride Matilda Shade, a "southern" belle of some repute. Leaving Matilda in Scotland with his family, Alexander travelled to Italy, Africa and India in accordance with the expectations of the times: as young men of means travelled widely in search of adventures and properties.[24] Being a dutiful husband however, he did have time to father two children between travels.

Harvey returned to Fergus with his family in 1842. Since he was both wealthy and related to Webster, he was able to purchase land adjacent to Fergus that belonged to his relatives. He called his domain "Kinnettles" after a village in Scotland close to where the Harvey family lived, and settled in with Matilda.

By 1860 Matilda had a beautiful stone home, complete with dairy, out-kitchens, servant quarters and a raceway. Its set-up was similar to what she had been accustomed to in one of the states sympathetic to the South. Nary a week went by that she did not hold a ball, a dinner party, a horse race or a soirée. While the Civil War raged in the United States, Matilda (Shade) Harvey played "The Belle of Kinnettles". Fergus was probably the better for it as some of the local Scots tended to be a straight-laced lot.

But all was not well in the Harvey compound as a series of events were to demonstrate. During a heated argument, one son shot and wounded his father. Soon after Alexander began to invest heavily in land in Northern Ontario. For her part, Matilda sent large sums of money south to the Confederate Army. By 1871 the Harvey's were financially strapped and unable to maintain their home. Ultimately they moved on in search of other fortunes and eventually settled in Western Canada.

Their land became the subject of a number of court actions and as a result, "Kinnettles, the Plantation of the North", sat empty for years. It was even reputed to be haunted by the ghost of a young woman whose body had mysteriously disappeared from the house. In the 1920's a tunnel was found that connected the house to the river. There two duelling pistols and riding spurs were discovered. It has been suggested that perhaps one of these pistols was used to wound Alexander. A male ghost was said to have been seen on a number of occasions inside the house and old blood-stained clothing was found under floorboards in the attic. All in all, the "secrets" of Kinnettles contain the potential of a good mystery.

Gilbert "Gibbie" Todd

Gibbie Todd was a close friend of James Webster. He set sail for Canada on the brig "Victoria" on August 29, 1836 with Thomas Webster, brother of James. Both arrived in Fergus on November 2, 1836, and as the old saying goes, the village was never the same again. Todd was described as "an impulsive man who occasionally lacked judgement but was earnest and honest."[25] In other words, Todd was a rascal.

His roles were many and varied. Over the years he clerked in Webster's store and took on the job of being a personal valet to Clephane, this job having the distinct advantage of access to an ample supply of whiskey at any hour of the day or night. He taught school at Allardice, went on to own a private school, became the first Clerk of the village and married three times. He also teamed store goods from Fergus to Egremont Township in Grey County. A Presbyterian, he led the congregational singing and played one of the few sets of bagpipes in Fergus.

Todd also kept the most interesting diary pertaining to Fergus and its inhabitants from 1836 to 1865.[26] His ability to consume the "cathur"[27] was legendary and he was always last to leave the tavern, any tavern. Gibbie's love for liquor led him to spend a memorable evening at "Bach Hall". After a tap had been left open inadvertantly on a keg of the finest, he began to lap the spilt contents up off the floor. Such talk went round about his exploits that he carved himself a square wooden cup which he carried attached to his belt, ready for action. In a tribute fitting that evening's memory, Todd would delight tavern patrons with his ability to lap his "cathur" from the cup rather than drink it in the usual fashion.

Clara Young

The reminiscences of Dr. Abraham Groves and Gilbert (Gibbie) Todd were kept alive throughout the years by both oral history and through a series of books, papers, diaries and journals. Few letters and journals written by women have been found as most women in the early 1800's were not schooled in reading, writing and arithmetic. Some could not sign

Clara's home, "Stonehome".

their names. However, James MacQueen, the first school master in Fergus was a person who insisted on equal education for both sexes. When he married, he taught his wife how to read. While there were several "ladies' academies" in Fergus that stressed the gentle arts, they dismissed math, science, Latin and Greek because they were considered to be of no importance to women.[28] Most women were socialized to wish for nothing more than to learn the arts of sewing, knitting, sketching and possibly reading. One exception was Clara Young.

Born in the 1850's and raised in a strict Victorian atmosphere, Clara set about to purposely break every written and unwritten law for Victorian women. Being a clever woman, she read avidly and became conversant on many subjects, continuing to educate herself at home while taking care of her father and sister.

However, to keep her father happy she also became an expert needlewoman. But she was known for her extensive collection of bugs and moths and her keeping of live birds, canaries being her favourites. At times she would have over one hundred on hand. In the summer these birds were allowed the freedom of large enclosed porches on her house. In the winter they were caged in one of the upstairs bedrooms. It is not surprising that she became known on St. David Street North as the "Bird Lady".

Although Clara was a tiny woman, almost birdlike in stature, she would walk the countryside late at night with no fear of attack or village talk. She befriended the less desirable "scarlet" women of the community, without becoming one herself. She nurtured the mind of any child that befriended her, yet did not marry. Being broadly self-educated, Clara understood Abraham Groves and his peers and was equal to them at any table they chose to share. It is through Clara and her inventive inquisitive mind and her penchant for writing that we have come to know more about early Fergus.

The Beatty Legacy

The Beatty name became synonymous with Fergus and with farm and household equipment around the world. Two brothers of Irish lineage, George and Matthew founded Beatty Bros. Limited in 1874, in the rented location of what was then known as the Temperance Hall on St. Andrew Street West. As soon as their sons, William and Milton, completed a suitable education in Toronto, they too joined the firm.

George Beatty.

The subsequent large manufacturing foundry would have a strong influence on Fergus for eighty-six years. The Firm, meaning the brothers, had a profound effect on the way their employees lived, where they worshipped, what they did or did not drink, what they did for recreation and, in a number of cases, who married whom.

Pity the employee who was caught with empty liquor bottles in a garbage pail! It was rumoured that even the garbage collectors were on the Beatty payroll. The Firm believed in temperance and made sure that Fergus remained one of the driest villages in Ontario. They were staunch Methodists, changing to the United Church at Union in 1925, and living by their own set of rules which included the following:

– lead exemplary lives to give employees a model to live up to

– give employees incentives to maintain their loyalties

– give employees recreational opportunities to take their minds off the evils of life

– build up-to-date products of real economic value

– foster good public relations by honest, efficient service

– have knowledge and experience relating to every phase of business and keep extensive equipment to meet the requirements of all operations

– have knowledge of basic ideals and principles upon which business and life are based.[29]

An example of their commitment to the community was their concern for proper employee housing for returning War Veterans. In 1919 Beatty Bros. formed the Fergus Housing Company Limited to build homes for employees at cost. Good building lots were made available for sixty dollars and house plans were provided. Local contractors went into agreements with the company to build homes, at the cost of the materials only, during their "off-season". The

W.G. Beatty.

company assisted the Veteran in financing the purchase of the house by deducting eighteen dollars per month off his pay. Eventually there were fifty homes and two apartment buildings erected, with some being built at the edge of the "acid pond", an oozing, bubbling swamp where the Firm spewed its liquid waste. These were constructed during the "off season" when the ground was frozen and didn't move beneath the feet of the workmen. Few people were environmentally conscious in the 1920's.

Winter was an especially difficult and trying time for the founders of Beatty Bros. The village of Fergus had an excellent curling club which had a reputation for playing a great game, and for drinking a great deal after the game. Many of the members of the club were also Beatty employees. After a Saturday night's game, all would gather at one house or another for "coffee and cake". Garbage collection day would find a poorly dressed man sorting through the refuse of the person who hosted the party. If bottles were found, problems awaited the fellow should he be an employee of the Firm! Employees quickly learned to bury suspect bottles. One enterprising fellow filled his neighbour's old outhouse with liquor bottles.

Several amusing stories are told about the hiring practises of the Firm. One elderly gentleman, who prefers to remain anonymous, said that when he was interviewed for a job he was asked if he drank. He replied that he didn't. He was asked if he smoked. He replied that he didn't. He was asked if he attended the Methodist Church. He replied that he did. He was hired. In fact, the fellow both smoked and drank. He began to attend the Methodist church the Sunday following his hiring. When asked if he didn't deceive the Beatty family, he said, "the fellow didn't ask if I lied. If he had I would have said... hell, yes!"

Another gentleman, who definitely must remain anonymous, began to date one of the daughters of the Firm with the sole purpose of obtaining a job. He was not of the same faith nor culture of the family. But he did manage to make enough of a nuisance of himself to eventually receive an invitation to dine with the family. During dinner he made sure he paid a great deal of attention to the daughter. She returned the attention, having a genuine liking for the fellow. After dinner, the young man was invited into the library for a chat. He was asked what it would take to leave their daughter alone. The young fellow replied, "A job for the rest of my life." His wish was granted. A notation found on his file stated ... "never fire or dismiss this man." He never dated the girl again, nor did he ever reveal the true nature of his attentions. She carried a flame for him for years, but he never went back on his word. He said that upon looking back he probably received the worst of the bargain. He was passed up for every promotion… he never received a decent wage increase… and he was given every dirty job in the plant. He did, however, have the pleasure of being able to smoke and drink whenever and wherever he pleased; although he never drank or smoked near the factory. Even he did not tempt fate.

The Firm, for all their eccentricities, were also well advanced in their promotion of sound business practises and for social programs for their employees. At a time when it was extremely rare for firms to deal in the two languages used in Canada (the 1920's) Beatty Bros. Limited had their salesmen's journals and materials printed in both English and French. They also offered French lessons to any employee who might be working in a French speaking country. They made sure that their advertising literature was printed in French and English for distribution not only in Quebec, but to the French West Indies, the Pacific Rim countries and French West Africa. They carved a niche for their products in the world marketplace by recognizing that communication in a second, and even third language was important for global success.

Social programs for employees included soccer and baseball teams.

Below: George Ernest Beatty with the Merv Wood Orchestra at Beatty Bros. 75th Anniversary Dance in the 1950's. Known as "George the Fourth", he was elected President of the family business in 1957 and died on April 10, 1961, at age 44. Right: Milton Beatty, Secretary and Sales Manager of Beatty Bros. Limited.

"A Family Affair for 87 Years", Beatty Bros. Limited. (Brigdens Limited, Toronto)

The Firm supported the arts by donating to the pipe band, the brass band and various community theatre and music groups. In June the Firm held an annual picnic in Victoria Park, an event which was looked on as the social occasion of the year. They held an annual Christmas party where all employee's children were fêted and fed. Their auditorium was ringed with colourful paintings of farm scenes, featuring Beatty equipment. These murals were painted by a member of their staff and were priceless! Regretably they disappeared in the 1960's, under coats of paint when new bosses took over. Perhaps someone will see the potential of these fantastic art histories of Fergus and Beatty Bros. Limited and will restore them to their former glory.

During the village's early years young people frequented a number of "swimming holes" on the Grand River – Birch Pool, Snakey, Mill Pond and Quarry Pool being the most popular. Although knowledgeable about Whirlpool and Mirror Basin some adventurous young folk even tempted fate by swimming there too. After a number of drownings, Beatty Bros. Limited approached Village Council, during the summer of 1929, about the possibility of erecting a swimming pool. The criteria they presented to council included the provision that they could build the facility on the

Even after public financing in 1929, the company was still Beatty controlled.

north corner of St. David and Queen Streets, beside the river and directly opposite their lower woodworking factory built c.1877. The firm insisted on this location in order to run heat and water pipes under the King's Highway from plant to pool. By utilizing heat from the factory the outdoor pools could be open from mid-April through mid-October. The

The Fergus Swimming Pool opened July 7, 1930. A product of the swimming programme, marathon swimmer Shirley Campbell (shown at left with her mother) made headlines in the 1950's. (Below) Bert Crockett with young swimmers, c.1943: on his knee, Billy Marsden and unknown; standing, Becky Russell, Eleanor Cunningham, Margaret Cunningham.

services of the pool and its instructor were to be offered to every child in the community under the same terms offered to employee's children.

Village fathers agreed that a swimming pool was an excellent idea. To facilitate a speedy opening, they quickly cleared all potential obstacles hindering construction. On July 7, 1930 the doors of Fergus Swimming Pool were opened to the general public. Under the capable direction of Bert Crockett, the pool's first instructor many fine swimmers were "graduated". One of the most notable is Shirley Campbell, who in the early 1950's attempted not one but two crossings of Lake Ontario. Three generations of Fergus children have learned to swim in this facility as the Beatty Bros. gift to Fergus is still operational today. The tunnel under the road and free heat from the Beatty factory were discontinued in the early 1960's when GSW Ltd. took over all Beatty Bros. facilities.

From Pens of the Past…

An interesting and accurate description of Hugh Black's tavern is found on a "for sale" advertisment flyer originally published February 10, 1846.

"The tavern is extremely well-adapted for carrying on the business of innkeeping. The building is a two storey, log structure. The ball room, one small parlour, the bar room, dining room and kitchen are on the ground floor. Thirteen bedrooms and a second parlour occupy the second floor. Besides Mr. Black's large family, thirty boarders are kept. The bar room is never empty – even on a Sunday."[30] Obviously this was long before Beatty's time in Fergus!

During Upper Canada's earliest years every man carried a stirrup cup known as a "Quaich". The hospitality of the day was that the first drink was

Templin's drawing based on a Fordyce sketch, c.1835: on the hill, the log school and St. Andrews Church; in the foreground, Black's Tavern and Young's Store.

always free, if the innkeeper was so inclined. Hugh Black kept a keg of whiskey on a stump outside his tavern. Travellers and villagers could have the first cup free. After that first drink they paid, but keep in mind that then whiskey was drunk like water. This public courtesy was given to men only. Women could have a drink, but they did so in the comfort of the parlour.

An Early Historian: W.F. MacKenzie

W.F. MacKenzie wrote a history of Wellington County in 1903 and included an excellent description of the village of Fergus.[31] This was the same year in which my grandmother moved to the community as a new bride, the only Italian family in the village. It is interesting to note that this historian gives a Mr. Scott, a member of the Black Pierpoint settlement, credit for the founding of Fergus. In the 1903 excerpt that follows, current street addresses of key sites identified by MacKenzie have been inserted for the benefit of today's reader.

The present prosperous Village of Fergus, so beautifully situated on the banks of the Grand River, with its handsome residences, and substantial stores, banks, etc; and surrounded by an agricultural country unsurpassed in the Province, was started some time in the fall of 1833, or the winter of '33 and '34. Its founder, probably was a Mr. Scott, whom the late A.D. Ferrier styled "The Contractor", and of whom no trace is now obtainable. With him were, evidently, associated during that winter Mr. James Webster, and Mr. Buist, styled "The Provost".

From his arrival on June 4, 1834, A.D. Ferrier played an important role in the life of his chosen village. As a chronicler of the past he recorded the growth of Fergus over a 30 year period. (Courtesy of Mrs. Alex Chambers)

On June 4th, 1834 Mr. Ferrier found just two houses, Mr. Scott's in which Messrs Webster and Buist lived; and Mr. Creighton's. From this humble origin has developed the present attractive village – a marvellous transformation have the intervening 72 years witnessed. A third house was being roofed. This house, known as Cleikum [sic] was afterwards occupied by Mr. Webster. Of this the contractor seems to have been Mr. C. Allan. During the summer a two storey log hotel was built on the site of the present American Hotel [301 St. Andrew Street West], known as Black's tavern, of which the genial proprietor was Hugh Black, formerly of Deanston, Perthshire, Scotland.

On the 30th of November, 1834 a St. Andrew's Society, long now extinct, was organized and continued its annual celebrations for many years.

Religious observances were not entirely neglected, for a start was made at the construction of St. Andrews Church in 1834, and it was completed the following year. In the meantime, Reverend Mr. Gale, the first ordained preacher, held services in the rather odd location of the big room in Black's tavern.

Mr. and Mrs. Ferguson (sic), who evidently believed the only sure foundation of prosperity must be based on the enduring principles of righteousness and morality, used their means and influence to secure for the "colony", of which they were the chief founders, both a church and a school. In 1837 Reverend Mr. Smellie arrived and became his successor, until the disruption, when he, in 1844 became attached to the Free Church and afterwards became pastor of Melville Church.

The Reverend George Smellie arrived from Scotland in 1843 and lived in a stone manse heated by four fireplaces. (Wellington County Museum and Archives)

In 1835 the school house was built and Mr. James McQueen, a good disciplinarian, possessing a good English and classical education became the teacher and continued for twenty-one years to discharge his duties and marked efficiency.

The summer of 1835 was a busy one in the settlement. Many new settlers were coming in, and new houses were required, and the little hamlet became a scene of great activity. A Mr. Walker started a bakery in 1835, and although his business was not very flourishing for some years, he proved a most estimable citizen, often supplying bread to those in need, for in those days pay day was an uncertain date in the future, as money was a thing rarely available. His log house stood for many years and his esteemed widow, who long survived him, died some time ago here.

This year, what could properly be called a store, was erected by Mr. Thos. Young, who became the proprietor, and kept a large assortment of splendid goods which he sold at prices considered reasonable at that time, owing to the difficulty and costs associated with conveying merchandise to the village. He was succeeded by Messrs, Watt and McGladdery, and later, by Mr. John Watt. The store stood opposite the American Hotel [site of the present Post Office].

The first grist mill was completed in the fall, the tenants being Messrs Mitchell and Gartshore, and the first grist was supplied by Mr. Buist, who reaped his first crop of wheat in 1835 which, although slightly frozen, made good seed, and was principally disposed of to the settlers for that purpose. The opening of the mill was celebrated in winter by a ball and supper, which

Mr. Ferrier described in "The Early Days of Fergus"[32] as "one of the merriest and funniest frolics ever I witnessed". Frequently, Mr. Ferrier referred to the over abundance of, and to free indulgence in, whiskey both Scottish and Canadian and no doubt its influence contributed to the merriment, as was generally the case on similar occasions. Messrs Mitchell and Gartshore manufactured oatmeal, so that during the first few years, owing to the wheat being frozen, the scones were rather tough, however, oatmeal cake, porridge, milk, venison, fish, potatoes etc. were obtainable, so that very few new settlements were as well supplied with necessaries in the early stages of their history as the Fergus colony.

At first mails were received once a week from Guelph, however, in 1836 the Fergus post office was established with Mr. Thomas Young as postmaster. In 1837 Mr. James McQueen was appointed and the duties of the office have ever since been efficiently performed by the MacQueen [sic] family.

In 1838, the Fergus Curling Club was organized, and the chieftains had two able and enthusiastic admirers of the game – "Provost" Buist and Mr. Hugh Black. The difficulty of procuring suitable "stanes" was overcome by Mr. Perry, an ingenious mechanic and a lover of curling, who contrived to make very good substitutes for the regulation granite ones out of solid maple blocks. These gave good satisfaction and continued to be used for years. This club continues to flourish and is now as popular as ever.

In 1838 Mr. Webster finished a new store, in which a large business was carried on for many years.

In 1836 a library was established, but was kept in existence only by the

Langsyne on the "Washing Green" Fergus, Ont.

"Gie me a canny draw through the port!"

"Hurray for the curlin',
Here's tae the curlin',
Hip-hip-hurras! for the game wi' the stanes,
The roar and the ring o't,
The dunt, and the ding o't,
The whirl, and the bir-r-ri, and the dirl o' the stanes." — *Weir*

St. Andrew Street West, c.1895. (Ontario Archives, S.6574)

Looking north up Tower Street, c.1895. (Ontario Archives, S-6583)

persistent efforts of Mr. Fordyce. When the Mechanics Institute was formed, the library was transferred to them, however, it did not prove to be a flourishing institution for a long time. Now Fergus has a fine public library which is currently under the charge of Mr. Unsworth.

In 1839 the principle buildings on what now constitutes the chief business centre of the village, St. Andrew Street, between Tower and St. David's Streets, were on the north side – Black's Tavern, J. Watt's store; Webster's dwelling on the site of the Commercial Hotel, J. Perry's house, Mr. McLaren's house, and two or three other houses. South of the street were the mill, a saw mill, a distillery, Webster's new store and Mr. Perry's shop.

The formation of the Fergus Rifle Company, in 1836, under the instruction of Sergeant Geor. Matthews, and the part it took in quelling the rebellion of 1837-38 is noted. A new organization under Col. Fergusson was started in 1838. From that time Fergus has had a company noted for efficiency, and one which still enjoys a proud reputation. For some years during the unsettled condition of the country after the rebellion, Fergus made little progress. In 1847 Schofield's map gives the village as possessing: two Presbyterian churchs – St. Andrews and Melville, two schools; two taverns – St. Andrew's Arms and the Fergus Arms; three stores, a flour oatmeal and barley meal mill, a saw mill, a distillery, a tannery, four shoemakers, five tailors, one saddler, four carpenters, three coopers, one turner, two stonemasons, one baker, two blacksmiths, one tinsmith and one watchmaker.

About this period the village began to make rapid and substantial progress. The northern municipalities were being rapidly settled and cleared, and farmers began to team their surplus grain and port to Fergus, Elora and Guelph. These were traded for goods or sold for cash, which in turn was invested in household necessities. The traffic created with the opening of the Fergus and Elora gravel roads, became extensive and important. In the years 1850 to 1860 many new families came to Fergus and by their enterprise the main business block on the front street became a center of considerable activity. Fine stores were erected, and Fergus assumed the smart appearance of a prosperous village. To this change Mr. Adam L. Argo contributed in no small degree for on renting the mills in 1852 he began to pay cash for grain. The late Henry Michie for many years one of the enter-

The Marshall Block, c.1895. (Ontario Archives, S-6566)

Looking south down St. David Street from St. George, c.1895. (Ontario Archives, S-6585)

prising businessmen, opened his store. Mr. Arch. McMullen, father of Senator James McMullen, and Reverend Dr. McMullen of Woodstock, built his store. Mr. James Grindley started his foundry on the site of the present Beatty Foundry, about 1854 [the Fergus Market site]. The Alma Block containing four shops, was erected, and in 1855 the American Hotel was rebuilt in stone as it now stands, [Canadian Imperial Bank of Commerce site]. The stone block south of St. Andrew occupied by Messrs Watt and Kerr was built in 1857. It was burned in 1859 and rebuilt in 1860 [to burn down again in the 1950's]. The Argo Block, built in 1859 still stands, a credit alike to the enterprise of the pioneer whose name it bears and to the village. On the corners of St. Andrew and St. David Streets are two buildings of more recent dates, fine structures built of Credit stone. Dr. Grove's, erected in 1880 [only partially standing in the 1990's as the imposing corner building was demolished by the Royal Bank in 1970 to make way for their present modern structure], and the Marshall Block, erected by Mr. John Black in 1883.

The village was incorporated in 1857 and sent the first representative,

Looking up St. David Street
from 101 St. Andrew
Street, c.1895.
(Ontario Archives
S-6580)

the late L. Wilkie to the County Council in 1858. This furnished the best possible evidence of the progress and increase of population during the years referred to previously. The year 1870 witnessed the formal opening of the Grand Trunk Railway to Fergus, and some ten years later came the Canadian Pacific Railway. It was anticipated that the opening of these thoroughfares of traffic would give an impetus to the development of the village. They certainly proved a boon, but it may be safely asserted that in no period in the history of the town was experienced the same boom as in the closing years of the fifties.

The schools of Fergus have always kept pace with the substantial character of the public institutions, business places and private residences of the place. The Public School, erected in 1866, has five teachers and the High School, built in 1877, has three. Besides these there is a separate school with one teacher. The schools have ample, well-kept grounds, and have a fine situation, unsurpassed in the village, with one exception, that of St. Andrews Church [both schools were stone buildings on the site of the present day James McQueen Public School]. St. Andrews and Melville churches had a common origin until the Disruption in Scotland in 1843, which led to the organization in Canada, in 1844, of the Presbyterian church in Canada, with which the Reverend Geo. Smellie, with a considerable majority of his congregation, decided to unite. The Old Melville

The persistence of the Honourable Adam Brown of Hamilton made possible the building of the Wellington, Grey & Bruce Railway. The first train arrived in Fergus in 1870. (A.C. Byerly)

CELEBRATION IN FERGUS.
Opening of the Wellington, Grey & Bruce Railway.

church [the building behind the tennis courts which Chas. Mattaini remodelled] was opened in March 1847. Afterwards it was improved and enlarged, and in this edifice the Reverend Dr. Smellie, completed 44 years of faithful services, rich in their influence for promoting and maintaining that righteousness which alone exalteth a nation. He died in Toronto in 1896. It was during the pastorate of the Reverend J.H. MacVicar, which began in 1896, that the present church was erected. Mr. Smellie's family were: William, dead; Dr. Thos. Smellie, ex M.P.P., Fort William: George, Vancouver, B.C.; Parker, Binscarth, Manitoba; Mrs. [Reverend] D.J. McDonnell, dead: and Miss Smellie, Fergus.

Those who remained faithful in their allegiance to the Church of Scotland continued to worship in St. Andrews. During the pastorate of the Reverend D.J. MacDonnell, afterwards for many years the able and the beloved pastor of St. Andrews, Toronto, the present St. Andrews Church and manse were completed. This church occupies what is conceded to be the finest site in Fergus. For 36 years this congregation has flourished under the pastoral care of the Reverend J.B. Mullan, whose discourses and addresses always characterized by reverent earnestness and interspersed with a vein of rich humour, and felicity of expression, peculiarly his own, have, not only in Fergus, but among the wide circle of his acquaintances, won for him deep and lasting esteem. His unique personality, his wholesouled sympathy, his deep interest in the temporal and spiritual welfare of the community and his large hearted generosity have endeared him to his people, who, with great respect, received the intimation of his intention to resign. He is no longer pastor of St. Andrews and Fergus feels his loss.

The Methodists, who have now a fine brick edifice, erected in 1869 [the corner of Maiden Lane and St. George Streets, now the site of James McQueen Public School] and a flourishing congregation, had no settled pastor here previous to 1861, when the Reverend A. Milligan was appointed to the charge of the church. The first church was built in 1852. Previous to that date services were for some years held in the schoolhouse.

Previous to the erection of the first St. James Anglican Church in 1858, services were held, for some years, in the Temperance Hall by the Reverend Mr. Smithurst of Elora, and his successor, Reverend C.E. Thomson. The first incumbent of Fergus received his appointment in 1867. The present neat edifice was erected in 1895 [now the United Co-operation of Ontario building which sits on the foundation of the church. Parts of the flying buttresses can still be seen].

St. Joseph's Roman Catholic Church, a substantial stone structure was erected in 1857. It is situated on a fine site. Services were held in connection with Elora.

There is also a Congregational Church, which is connected with the Church at Speedside and the Plymouth Brethren have a place of meeting.

Fergus is now, a fine, substantial, up-to-date village of about 1,500 popu-

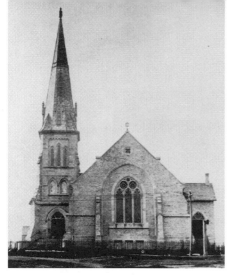

St. Andrews Church has the distinction of occupying the most prominent site in Fergus. (Ontario Archives, S-6563)

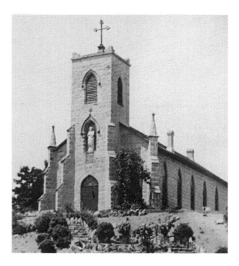

St. Joseph's Church. This Roman Catholic church dates back to the early days of Fergus, founded in 1844.

St. James Anglican Church, at the corner of St. Patrick and Tower Streets, c.1900.

Bridge, blacksmith shop, Melville United Church and American Hotel, c.1934.

Mrs. W.G. (Martha) Beatty shown in 1930 ceremony observing the addition to Melville United Church.

Looking north west from 101 St. Andrew Street West, c.1895. (Ontario Archives S-6565)

lation showing evidences of the general prosperity Canada has been enjoy-
ing for some years, having modern achievements such as electric lighting,
cement walks, etc.

The facilities for shipment – afforded by the railways, and the superior
stock produced in the vicinity, together with the enterprise of the local buy-
ers, give Fergus a reputation for the shipment of cattle, sheep etc., that rivals much larger centres. One of the evidences of prosperity the visitor to
Fergus cannot fail to observe is the large number of large handsome, modern residences, with well kept lawns, whose attractiveness is enhanced by
their pleasing situation that may be seen in several parts of the town.

Among the public institutions, industries and business places must be

Monkland Mills, shown here c.1895, was operated for almost 70 years by James Wilson
and his son of the same name.

mentioned the Royal Alexandra Hospital, a beautifully situated, well equipped institution, the property of Dr. A. Groves, open to the public. The foundry of Beatty and Sons; the Fergus and Monkland Mills of Jas Wilson and Sons, established in 1856; Templin Carriage Works; the Massey-Harris agency of R. J. Brown; the implement agency of G.D. Groves, ex-reeve of the village; the Egg Emporium of W. Richardson and Sons; the Fergus Cold Storage building; and John Chapman's Farming Implement establishment are major contributors. There are two firms doing a good business as furniture dealers and undertakers, R.A. Curliss in the fine and long established Argo Store and John Thomson and Son. The fine and well equipped drug and stationery store of S.R. Davey, successor to R. M. Glenn, is found in the long established business of R.H. Perry in the McQueen Block. In this line, also, there is the long established and up-to-date store of R. Phillip & Son, drugs, stationery, fancy goods etc. Fergus has two departmental stores doing a large business, both of which would compare favorably with city stores. They are commodious, up-to-date in equipment and arrangement, and carry an extensive and varied stock. The proprietors are Steele Bros., and Jas Russell. One of the pioneer business establishments is the general store of James Pattison & Co. The Fergus Goldsmith Hall of S. Marshall, jeweller, optician etc., is an establishment rarely equalled outside of large centres and one of which Fergus may be proud. The hardware stores are those of John Mennie and A.E. Nichols. Mr. Mennie has been in business for himself for

The Templin Carriage and Waggon Works c.1910. (Wellington County Museum and Archives)

Morrow's drugstore.

twenty-seven years. He has been familiar with the progress of Fergus since his boyhood, and is, probably, the best authority still living on the early settlement and development of the village. The writer found him genial and entertaining and an hour spent in his office was both helpful and enjoyable. The tailoring establishments are those of W.C. Dass, Thomas Milne and W.A. Ross. John Moffatt has for many years been the chief contractor. The grocery, flour, feed and fruit store of Armstrong Bros., J.A. Carton, boots, shoes, groceries etc., J. McBeath, boots and shoes, C.M. Post, tobacco, confectionery, groceries etc.; H.L. Harrison, boots and shoes; McClannaghans tin ship; and Robert Kerr stoves and tinware are to be noted, as well as the fancy and millinery store of Miss Bonthron. R. Craig, musical instruments; James Calder, clocks and watches; the bakeries of A.H. Foote and W.A. Jackson; A and T Mill and Robert Gow, butchers; Fitzpatricks and McDermott's harness shops; the Armstrong, Wm. McDermott and George Robinson liveries; the Fergus Marble Works of John Alpaugh & Son; the coal and wood yards of T. J. Hamilton and Chas. Mattaini; and the elevator of J. Wilson & Sons are all flourishing in their respective lines of business. G.A. Reid, dentist, belonging to one of the pioneer families, has a large practice in his line. There is, too, the photograph gallery of James Walker. There are four good hotels – The Commercial, the Wellington, the Murphy House and the American. Banking facilities are afforded by the Imperial Bank, established in Fergus in 1878, and the Traders Bank.

There are, at least, three streets in Fergus commemorative of early settlers. Tower Street, which bears the name of the Hon. Adam Fergusson's

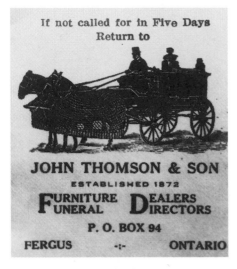

If not called for in Five Days
Return to

JOHN THOMSON & SON

ESTABLISHED 1872

FURNITURE **D**EALERS
FUNERAL **D**IRECTORS

P. O. BOX 94

FERGUS -:- **ONTARIO**

From an envelope of John Thomson &
Son. (Wellington County Museum and
Archives)

second wife; Provost Lane, the pioneer Buist; and Maiden Lane, in honour of Miss Inglis, a sister of Squire Inglis of the Paisley Block, Guelph, the chimney of whose house is still standing and was pointed out to me by John Gerrie. The house which was only burned a few years ago, stood opposite Mr. M. Anderson's.

Victoria Park, laid out some ten years ago, with its well made track one-third of a mile long, its large grandstand and band stand, its skating rink, is used by the Centre Wellington Agricultural Society for exhibition purposes and its fine ground inside of the track for playing lacrosse is a feature of which the people may well feel proud. The park is beautifully situated, and the rising ground in the rear is planted with trees, which will in a few years then to make this a most attractive resort. [This is the same park that several groups in the community wished to "improve" in the early 1990's by making a portion of it into a paved parking lot for high school students. Sanity prevailed, but the issue is far from dead!]

Inside Russell's store.

The *Fergus News Record*, an ably edited and a well conducted news weekly journal, of which the proprietor is Mr. J.C. Templin, is the only paper now published in the village. To the obliging editor the writer is indebted for assistance generously proffered, and for access to the Christmas number of the News Record for 1902, an issue of twelve pages, containing excellent well written sketches of "Fergus Past and Present", by the editor. It was printed on good paper and contained numerous illustrations, and was altogether the most creditable issue, the production of which must have cost no little expenditure of labour and money. If history repeats itself, Fergus shall continue to prosper and grow without losing its gentile, cultured appearance, its industrious nature and its Scotch background."[33]

A self-styled County historian, W. F. MacKenzie collected information on villages and towns in Wellington County for a number of years. In 1903, while residing in the area, he did a series of "sketches" on local areas, including this one about Fergus. While his write-ups were considered most accurate and up-to-date at the time, he did tend to dwell heavily on church history, an aspect considered most important since the fabric of many communities was bound together by the strength of their churches.

M.C. Schofield: Cartographer and Artist

By 1845 Fergus was ready for expansion, but Webster and Fergusson were running out of relatives to lure to Fergus. Thus, M.C. Schofield was hired to provide a map and sketches suitable for an advertising circular which could be posted in various places in Upper and Lower Canada and in Scotland. Schofield did an admirable job. His short description of the community is most enlightening:

Fergus is situated in a fine agricultural section of the province; which will soon be completely opened up; as companies were incorporated by the act of the Provincial parliament, last session, for the construction of plank, macadamized roads from Dundas to Guelph, and from Guelph to Fergus [some 1990's wags will say no money has been spent on #6 highway since]. And a line of Railway from Toronto to Goderich passing through Fergus was surveyed during the present year [1847], a bill for which was passed. There are two Presbyterian churches in Fergus; the one [St. Andrews Church] connected with the synod, in connection with the established church in Scotland. The other [Melville Church] in connection with the Presbyterian Synod of Canada. There are also two well conducted schools, one of which has been in operation since the formation of the settlement, and the other

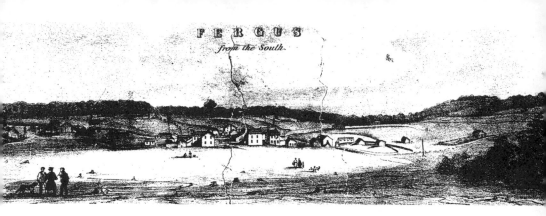

A view of Fergus from Schofield's plan.

[for girls] was established last year. There is a post three times a week between Fergus and Guelph. A stage runs regularly on the same days; in addition to which extras are furnished whenever required."[34]

A Letter from Clara Young

It is interesting to read about life in a village from a woman's perspective. Many of the women who emigrated to Upper Canada had limited formal education and therefore did not write letters or keep journals. Fergus was fortunate because a number of woman residents did keep journals, diaries and their personal letters. This is possibly so because a high percentage of men in the community had university educations and married women with some education. As previously noted Clara Young was a clever young lady. She obtained as much education as she could from village schools and continued her self education at home. She wrote numerous letters to her aunts, many of which were returned to "Stonehome" some years ago. Clara was a succinct writer who could tell more in two short paragraphs than many men did in thirty.

> I walked to the main area today to purchase sugar. If it were not for the mud holes one must walk around, and the pigs one must avoid, the walk would be a pleasant one. I planted iris root; father considers iris an ugly plant, but it was given by a friend and I could not put it on the compost. I like iris.
>
> The river ran high today after the rains of the last three days. I could not wade across at my usual place, but had to use the bridge to get to the hill on the south side, where I watched the village for a very long time, remembering what it was like when I first came. The Reverend Smellie was in his garden working with his man. There are 200 souls in the village now which I consider to be very exciting. Tomorrow I will walk to the main area again as a new store is introducing itself....[35]

Earthwatch of the Early Days…

Early records were kept by various residents who used a weather station located on Queen Street East behind the old hospital. Reverend Patrick Bell also kept records of temperature and precipitation. What both sets of records do is confirm the suspicion that "everything old is new again."

The 1830's were noted for the amount of snow which fell, although between 1835-37 there was no sleighing until January, because of lack of snow cover. These years were some of the coldest on record. It is agreed by all weather watchers that the summer of 1838 exceeded all records for being hot and dry, it was a summer such as the one in 1988, one hundred and fifty years later. That year the riverbank in the settlement caught fire and burned from Tower Street to the Base Line (Gartshore/Scotland Streets). No dwellings were destroyed, but because of the peaty nature of the bank, the fire burned underground in some places for several days.

The settlement endured a seven year span of droughty conditions in the 1860's. The cause, the settlers felt ,was the extensive clearing of the land, which led to the drying up of small streams and bogs. It would seem that we have not learned much from our forefathers. Here we are in the 1990's still clearing bog land and creating problems!

The longest recorded winter Fergus experienced was in 1842-43 when snow began to fall in September and did not leave until June. The year of 1843 became known as the year of no summer as there were frosts every month of that year. In the 1970's our area experienced a similar winter when snow began to fall on Thanksgiving weekend and was still around in great quantities on April 15. The last frost during that year was June 13.

The most severe winter of all was from 1855 to 1856 when temperatures rarely rose above ten degrees Fahrenheit, even during the day. This record was not broken until 1917. However, the worst storm Fergus ever experienced in the twentieth century was in the winter of 1947 when seven feet of snow fell over a two-day period.

The warmest winter experienced in Fergus was from 1932 to 1933, when there was no snow cover until February and when it rained for seventeen consecutive days in January. One woman remembers attending a funeral in January and seeing the coffin float on water in the bottom of the grave. The winter of 1994 to 1995 is also considered to be one of the warmest.

Housekeeping during the early settlement years was interesting, especially when one considers the impact of differing weather conditions. Meat was hung up in the rafters after it was smoked or salted. In most homes, it froze during the winter months and did not spoil, although smoking usually preserved meat as well. To thaw the meat, it was placed in a box in a clear, swift running stream for a number of hours. If a person was not sharp, they could lose their Sunday roast to a prowling bear or wolf!

If the doors and windows of the log cabin were not tightly closed, water froze in vessels and bread would freeze sitting on the table. When the fire went out one could expect that every bit of food in the house would be frozen, except that which was stored under the flooring – if the cabin had flooring. Stone dwellings offered little more protection. The second storey of most stone homes was not heated. A cup of water froze on a windowsill. During the coldest weather, a fire was kept burning in the stove twenty-four hours a day. Stoves were, as mentioned, preferred over fireplaces.

Because cold was normal and tolerated as part of life in Scotland, it was not considered a nuisance here until people became accustomed to central heating. Settlers were a hearty lot of people, taking snow on their bedcovers for granted. As efficient stoves became more common place and houses better built, people began to suffer the common cold. The cause was diagnosed accurately by an early doctor;... "too much hot to cold; cold to hot", he said "Do not leave a hot house for a cold day nor enter a hot house from a cold day".[36]

Although tornadoes are considered a recent phenomenon by some people, evidence does exist to show that they were just as likely to occur in the past as they are today, not that they are that frequent in our area. Newspaper accounts and journals mention that settlers came across acres of land where "it seemed the hand of God had flattened every tree in the same direction for a mile or so."[37] In one journal it mentioned five areas, between Fergus and Guelph, parallel to each other and four miles between each where "the earth seems to have thrown the trees from the west to the east as if in disgust at their presence."[38] In the 1960's five small "tornadoes" came across the area, two below Fergus, three to the north of the community. Although not identified as tornadoes by the weather office, as a result of their presence, trees were laid on their side from west to east. More recently in the 1980's the area was swept by tornadoes, the same band that swept through Grand Valley and Barrie. Three areas were extensively damaged, all to the north of the Fergus community. It is interesting to note that back in the 1860's settler's diaries mention violent windstorms which they called cyclones, sweeping across the province during a three day periods.

During the month of September 1870 the villagers wakened up to the earth moving or rather shaking under their feet. The movement did not cease for thirty days; sometimes a gentle shaking, enough that a ball could be kept bouncing on the floor; sometimes a rocking sensation; once or twice enough to throw dishes from a sideboard; sometimes sufficient to rattle dishes and pictures for three to four hours at a time. Some "experts" thought that the water flowing over the dams was setting up a rhythmic movement, but this was found not to be true when the water was lowered in both dams. The phenomenon was never repeated. Fergus has had several little shocks in the 1920's and again in the 1960's – just enough to rattle a picture or two on a wall and to set the nerves a "jingling".

Provost Lane in a 1947 snowstorm.

Theatre, Music
and Sporting Features

The good people of Fergus have always been an active lot – whether direct participants or appreciative audiences. The culture of the community is deeply rooted in events of the past and lovingly preserved for those of the future.

From Drill Shed to Theatre on the Grand

Theatre in Fergus, as in other small communities, has experienced "peaks and valleys". Until the 1850's when a proper stage was installed in the Drill Shed, there was no place suitable for the presentation of professional theatre. When the hall was completed, James Grindley, who owned and operated a foundry (now the site of the Fergus Market), introduced theatrical productions to Fergus. Although Mr. Grindley made an effort to run the foundry, his first love was theatre. In Scotland he had been an actor of some note. It has been said that his love of theatre was only superseded by his penchant for wetting his whistle.

A good stage spurred Grindley into action. Each year he chose a suitable play, found actors of the male gender only, manufactured scenery and props and immersed the community and area in excellent productions. Because there was a lack of women, especially young females who wished to "take to the stage", he was forced to cast young men in the roles that normally women would perform. This did not seem to bother the young fellows who enthusiastically lined up to audition.

Although the plays went off without a hitch, they usually went off without Mr. Grindley, who spent his time under the stage in the jail cell,

SUMMER THEATRE AT THE GRAND presents

Three One-Act Plays:

Voice of the People
by Robertson Davies
Directed by Gary Bryant

Curtains
by Gloria Gonzales
Directed by Gerry Butts

Not Enough Rope
by Elaine May
Directed by L. Pieper

Grand Theatre,
Fergus

July 22nd, 23rd, 24th
July 28th, 29th, 30th, 31st

8:00 p.m.
Tickets: $5.00

Phone 843-2050

drunk. He always managed to see the actors through every rehearsal without hitting the bottle, but he could never make a performance in a sober state. There was a trap door on stage which opened to the basement. At the end of each performance, when Grindley's name was called to "take a bow" he would stick his head and shoulders up through the trap door and bow low, hitting his head on the floor of the stage. This performance was avidly awaited by all in attendance.

Grindley delighted in spoofing newcomers to the community. He would feign deafness and, being a master of the English language, could always misinterpret their questions. When he sold the Foundry, he would leisurely walk to Guelph and take the stagecoach or hitch a ride with a teamster back to Fergus. He would check to see who might be on the stage before he bought a ticket. Should there be someone new to the area, he purchased a ticket immediately. If not, he found an obliging teamster. Many a new settler's first introduction to Fergus was through Mr. Grindley, who gave them fifteen miles of absolute nonsense! If they endured Grindley's first assault, they were recommended for "citizenship".

Grindley eventually moved to Toronto, but his legacy of theatre was kept alive by a group of individuals who made sure the stage in the town hall was well used. During the 1880-90's rarely a week went by that there wasn't something presented.

After the First World War, love for live theatre seemed to wane. There were no James Grindley's to champion the stage. Disinterest in theatre led to disinterest in the Drill Shed and eventually productions ceased.

The Grand Theatre, which is one of the finest stone structures erected in Fergus, was built in 1928 by Samuel Fardella. Originally from Palermo Italy, Sam ran a fruit and flower shop in Fergus for a number of years before he seized the opportunity to take advantage of the new rage – movies. No expense was spared to make the theatre the best in the area. To hedge his bets, Sam installed a stage; just in case moving pictures bombed and vaudeville returned. The theatre's accoustics were and still are excellent. One of the first movies to play at the Grand Theatre was "Ramona". Several women were so impressed by this film that they named new babies after the heroine. I always thought that Ramona was a very romantic name – but by the time I came along, my mother had other names in mind.

The Grand Theatre was the meeting place for three generations of Fergusites, many of whom will never forget the matron who patrolled the aisles to make sure no hanky-panky was going on in the back row!

This enterprise was a family operation. Both Mrs. Fardellas, Sammy's first wife had died in 1939, and his five daughters worked the box office and "in house". The first projectionist was Fred Pearse. Sam's only son, Tony (Anthony) Fardella, apprenticed under Fred and eventually took over the job. As my father was a close friend of Tony, we were allowed upstairs while he rewound the reels after the show. Tony was a generous man who loved to treat us to Saturday afternoon matinees. He would watch for us to arrive and escort us to the coin operated candy machine where we could choose a treat. Tony was a bachelor who said he did not need a woman in his life as his huge motorcycle "took as much attention as a wife". He drove his bike all over Ontario and the northern United States. When I was a child, the thrill of being allowed to sit on Tony's motorcycle was only surpassed by the latest Gene Autrey western playing at the Grand Theatre.

Motor cars contributed to the demise of the Grand. During the 1960's people thought nothing of driving to larger centres for entertainment. As Sammy Fardella was a man of principles who refused to bring some of the more violent shows into the theatre, this meant that those into "blood and guts" went elsewhere. Unable to compete, the theatre showed its last movie around 1962. The building was sold in 1970 and was used as the headquarters for a Cable TV company. It also became home for

theatrical productions which were performed by local amateur theatre
groups, the most notable being the
Elora Community Theatre Group.
Gradually the threatre building dete-
riorated to the point where it was
questionnable how long it could survive without major expensive repairs.

Various projects were developed for
the building, but none of them were
compatible with movies or live theatre. Fortunately, the vision of two far
sighted individuals, Hugh and Lor-
raine Drew-Brook saved the building.
They invested thousands of dollars of
their own money into fully restoring
the building's tin ceiling, seats, stage,
terrazzo floor and art deco interior design. Theatre on the Grand was re-

Anthony (Tony) Fardella with author's elder sister Madelyn Mattaini
in July 1941.

opened for professional summer theatre in 1993. Today the community is
proud of this non-profit organization dedicated to the preservation of
both the building and live theatre in Fergus.

Music to Soothe the Soul

The Fergus Brass Band was established in 1855, just before the Fenian
raids. When men from Fergus were mustered and marched to Guelph
they did so to the beat of the Fergus Fife and Drums, the forerunner of the
present Fergus Brass Band. Since 1949 the band has been under the capable leadership of Art Lee. The bandmaster and this extraordinary
group of individuals bring the joy of music to a large number of people.
Their existence is due largely to the financial support coming from the
generosity of the townspeople. In 1919 when a canvas was made to raise
funds for a bandshell, all but one businessman gave the prescribed dona-
tion of one dollar. He was forgiven for... "as Fergus is a Scots town and
this man is a very conservative Scots man, it is understandable."[39]

The band is always willing to play for the community and rarely turns
down a request for "music, please". One story about their generosity in
return comes to mind. In 1984 Paul and Villie Vlachos were celebrating

Fergus Brass Band 1991. Back row l to r.: Art Lee, Frank Dawson, Bob Snyder, Bill French, Des Rooney, Roy Hurlbut, Glen Donaldson, Mark Wettlaufer, Bob Skeoch, Ken Plante. Center: Jim Maguire, Paul Smid, Gary Nijenhuis, Paul Landoni, Lorne Service, Peter Harris, Dale Gear, Wayne Prine, John Krywan, Wes Ryckman, Merv Woods. Bottom: Doug Hall, Steve Wilde, Bill Coulter, Bill Brown, Ray Pearse, Gordon Padfield, Dave Spaetzel, Henry Spoelstra, Bob Ennis. Absent: Dean Earngey, Jack MacDonald, Jack Steuernol, Rodger Gatehouse. (Courtesy of Art Lee, Band Master)

fifty years in the restaurant business in Fergus. During this time the couple had enjoyed the respect of their community. When asked what they wanted most for their anniversary, Villie asked quietly that the band should play as a surprise for Paul. The businessmen organized a surprise party on a Saturday and promptly at 11:00 a.m. the Fergus Brass Band marched up to the door of the Fergus Restaurant to serenade Paul. Villie had made her request only on Thursday and the band had a commitment out of town on Saturday at noon, but true to their community spirit they played for Paul and "drove like bats out of hell" to get to their next engagement. Art Lee, the undisputed best, darn bandmaster in the world, just could not resist a surprise party!

One woman, who shall remain unnamed, lived an interesting and eccentric life in a small cottage on Union Street East. She had no love for the village women, considering them gossiping, mean-spirited individuals. However, she held the most spectacular and innovative birthday parties, inviting all her male friends. At one of her most memorable occasions, she welcomed all the menfolk in the village, including the Fergus Brass Band. All responded with enthusiasm, after all her parties were the talk of the town for the year. Some didn't tell their wives where they were

Fergus Pipe Band in 1947: Back row: Percy Gibson, Joe Fletcher, Reg Manley, Matt Patterson, Scotty Henderson, Phil MacDonald, Jimmy Wilson, Jack Cameron, Jim MacKenzie, Jack Fair, Lloyd Osborne. Front row: Ivan Ostic, Russell Tuck, Dick Fletcher, Eugene Landoni, Freddi Smith, Doug Keir, Cliff Oakman. 1947 was first time the band wore this MacKenzie Military style jacket. Absent: Henry Woods, Bob Heron, Louie Mason. (Courtesy Jim MacKenzie)

going, knowing how the women felt about "Mrs. Eccentricity". During the festivities several photographs were taken and one mysteriously appeared in the *Fergus News Record*. That evening when the paper came out there were many men who were served "hot tongue" for supper.

The Fergus Pipe Band was organized in 1927 by J.C. MacDonald and J.W. Henderson. As both of these men belonged to the Seaforth Highlanders in Scotland, the tartan they chose for the band was that of their regiment, the MacKenzie. By canvassing the merchants and industry, enough money was raised for eight pipers' uniforms and four drummers' uniforms. It was decided that each piper would be responsible for purchasing his own set of pipes, at ninety-three dollars per unit. In 1927 that $93.00 was a fortune! Most men were making less than twelve dollars a week. The band nearly did not get off the ground, but a sympathetic bank manager gave the group a loan so that all eight sets of pipes might be ordered from Scotland. Fundraising became a must! A hot dog stand was set up between #245 and #247 St. Andrew Street West and staffed by volunteers. One and one-half years later the loan was paid off.

The Fergus Pipe Band is an integral part of the community. Some of the members have been with the band for over fifty years, almost the life

Recent photos of the Fergus Pipe Band: Active members – Pipers: P.M. Bob Dewar, P.S. Sam Harrop, P.S. Dean Percy, P.S. Nigel Moore, Kristi Ashton, Heather Buchanan, Bill Coish, Michelle Dewar, Rob Dobie, Matt Glendinning, Chad Green, Fran Lawrie, Ian Matheson, Clarence McCallum, Joy McNichol, John Pope, Don McAlpine. Drummers: D.S. Kevin Ashton, Jan Anderson, Morley Ashton, Denise Dewar, Yvette Dewar, Betty Henderson, Brad Kent, Alan Laing. (Courtesy Anita L. Dewar)

of the band. No celebration in Fergus would be complete without both Fergus bands.

Early Sports: Lacrosse and Curling

Lacrosse was first played in Fergus in 1868 when the Lightfoot Lacrosse Club was formed. The game, called "Baggataway" by the Algonquins and "Weewaarathon" by the Iroquois, is a fast-paced, dangerous game if one does not know what one is doing. In 1882 the name of the Club was changed to the Fergus Thistles, a name still associated with lacrosse in Fergus. Lacrosse aficionados will remember Jack Russell, Tom Russell, Red Brown, John Joe Atkinson, Blyth Brown, Flick Graham, Sandy Russell, Walter Smart, Neil Mattaini, Bucko McDonald and Eric White.

The author has attended only one lacrosse game in her life. Her great aunt, a gentile delicate woman from London, insisted on seeing a lacrosse game in the 1950's. This particular game happened to be one of the bloodiest of the season, fought between the Brantford Mohawks and the Fergus team. The Great Auntie spent the evening on her feet throwing verbal abuse at both teams. The author spent her time being physically ill. Lacrosse is the third oldest sport in Fergus superseded only by Scottish Heavy Athletic events and by curling.

The Fergus Curling Club was established in 1834 and is the oldest continuous curling club in Ontario. Early games were played among the stumps on St. Andrew Street. Later games were played at the washing green on the river. As the river ice was unpredictable, tournaments and special matches were held at the Beaver Meadow west of Garafraxa Street.

Members of the 1943 Fergus Curling Club. Front row, left to right: J. Morrice, H. Mann, L. Fatum. Back row: F. Thacker, Dr. G. Sutherland, L. Gear, Red Marshall, "Miff" Simpson, George Graham, M. Bakke.

Provost Buist and Hugh Black were avid curlers, but always played on opposing sides. Each year the club celebrated the end of the season with a beef and greens supper (complete with appropriate libations) in the Drill Shed. Even the Beatty brothers could not persuade the curlers to become upholders of temperance. During prohibition in the 1920's a problem developed concerning the "libations". Charlie Mattaini was invited to join the Curling Club, an Italian at a Scottish sport! This was a prudent move on behalf of the curling club for Charlie could supply the "lubricant" that kept the curlers operational, the dinner traditional and everyone in good spirits, so to speak. Surprise, of surprises, Charlie could curl and became a valued member of the team. Charlie first made his

Charles Mattaini.

An historic bowling scene, c.1920. The late David Rea, J.P. of Fergus engaging at his favourite sport. Reading left to right: Col. Hamilton, Richard Pith, William Burr, T.J. Hamilton, William McAlister. (A.C. Byerly)

"libation" in the old Melville Church building and later moved the still to his lumberyard on the east corner of Albert and Tower Streets. While everyone knew he made wine, few suspected he also had a still!

Curlers in Fergus take their game seriously. Do not ask them to miss their curling night. Die if you must, but after you've completed your game if you please! Provost Buist would be pleased at the dedication to the ancient sport displayed by players today. As a reminder of the early days, one of the original maple wood curling stones, designed by the mechanic Perry in 1838, is on display at the Curling Club along with other interesting bits of club history.

Exotic Oranges, Ghosts
and Other Oddities

Mrs. Foote, a woman who lived to be well over one hundred years of age, and who remembered the earliest days of the settlement, is credited with stories told to the author's grandmother who was a young girl in Fergus in the 1890's. One such story involves the exotic oranges.

The golden globes appeared in John Ironside's window on a Thursday morning in December of 1868. There were twenty-four of them. Some people didn't know what they were, but they were soon told by those lucky few who had tasted one, that they were oranges. By Thursday afternoon, nearly everyone in the village had walked past Mr. Ironside's window at least once to gaze on the exotic fruit. Several even ventured into the store to ask how much one might sell for. Mr. Ironside's answer was always, "I haven't made up my mind yet".

On Thursday evening the oranges were moved to the back of the display and covered so they would not freeze. Friday morning they were once again the central attraction in the window display. By Friday afternoon word had spread throughout the surrounding countryside that John Ironside had twenty-four oranges for sale.

"Knowing Ironside, the price will be so high no one will be able to afford more than one," a fellow was heard to grumble. John Ironside was known for driving a hard bargain.

By Saturday afternoon the village had more than its share of farm families in town to shop. They stood before John Ironside's window to peek at the tropical wonders. When anyone asked, Mr. Ironside replied, "They'll be gone from the window at 6:00 p.m." Of course, the crowd began to gather in the shop well before six o'clock.

"What are you going to do, John" Hold an auction"

When no more people could fit into the store, John Ironside sat himself down on his counter and announced to the crowd that the women and children should step forward, children first. A murmur went through the assembly. Ironside then asked who had tasted an orange. Half a dozen hands went up out of the fifty or so people gathered.

"I am going to peel these oranges and give each of you a piece. It is only right that the children be the first to taste the fruit, followed by the women, then the men. Do you not agree?"

"He must be daft in the head," one fellow was heard to say. "He could get one dollar apiece for each."

John Ironside carefully peeled the first orange and placed the peel on a paper behind him. He separated the luscious, juicy sections and handed them around. He repeated the same process with the remaining twenty-three fruits. No one went without a piece. Everyone savoured their taste of the tropics.

"You're a good man, John Ironside."

Ironside explained it was a Christmas present to them.

After everyone had dispersed, he carefully wrapped the peelings. He measured out ten pounds of sugar, left the shop in the capable hands of his assistant and hurried home. If he was early enough, his wife and her maid would turn the peelings into candied orange rind before the Sabbath began at midnight. On Monday morning he would have the delicious confection for sale, and would make three times the money he would have, had he sold the oranges themselves. Canny Scot, or what!

While judgement may be reserved on the existence of ghosts, the following stories are presented for your enjoyment. No book would be complete without a ghost story – or two. Over the years stories such as the following have become part of the folklore of Fergus.

The old man walking silently back and forth in the parking lot at the hospital is not to be pitied. Although he has his grey and balding head down, and is wearing an old fashioned black suit, if he would look you straight in the eye – well, you would be gazing into a pair of brilliant blue, intelligent eyes. Those eyes and that "body" belong to Abraham Groves. But you must not disturb the man. For you see he is not really there. Or is he? The good doctor seems to be walking the corridor of his old hospital, but what is he looking for? No one knows. One man was so sure he had hit a living being, he leapt from his car and looked under the front and back wheels. He then turned to a man standing beside him in the lot ask if he would take a look – only to have the man fade away before his very eyes.

There is a very old stone house on Queen Street where the residents frequently experience "someone" sitting on their bed at night. This takes place in a second floor bedroom. Former residents of the house report the sighting of a man in the basement – in the east corner of the basement. In a century old stone home on St. David Street a young boy appeared occasionally at the door of one of the upstairs bedrooms. This bedroom is also located on the east side of the house.

On the northwest side of Fergus there used to be a large beaver meadow, which was alive with the wild creatures of the woods – fox, deer, raccoon, mud turtle; and which was even richer with wild indigenous plants and trees. For generations this was a summer campground and a winter hunting ground of Indians. Native families came to pick berries, dry venison and make black ash and basswood storage baskets which they would trade with villagers. Their campfires could be seen in the village. Often the Perry house would host a group of these migrant natives, who traded goods for oats, flour, tea and cloth. Singsongs were accompanied by drums. When the mists were heavy on the meadow and the light was right, people walking the railway line in the 1940's swore that they could see the campfires of the Indians and hear the drums. Some attributed the phenomenon to swamp gas and bullfrogs. Was it? Or did the Native Indians retain their ancient claim to the land?

In April of 1879, Charles Kay was walking the riverbank at Kinnettles, the Alexander Harvey House, when he came across the body of a young woman which had obviously been there for some time. He notified the Fergus Coroner and found a group of men to remove the body to the empty Harvey House. Because the winter had been long and cold, the body was in remarkable condition. It was placed on a table in the abandoned house until a full inquiry could be conducted the following morning. During the evening a number of people viewed the remains, but none recognized the woman. No one was left to watch over the remains and of course, the body disappeared overnight. Good bodies were hard to come by. Medical students needed a skeleton for their studies and grave robbers abounded in the area.

It was ascertained that the body was that of a young girl who had escaped from the Poor House one half mile away, wearing nothing but a flimsy nightgown. But where did the body go? Who took it? No one knew, or better yet, no one said they knew.

In May, patrons at the Wellington Hotel complained about a servant girl who insisted on entering their room at night. She was pretty enough, dressed in a nightgown and spoke not a word. This occurrence was repeated night after night until August of that year when the mysterious servant girl vanished. A young servant girl in the room of a rough teamster was not unwelcome, but when they made a grab for her, their arms went right through her! She was spotted again in a small house near the Wellington Hotel in the early 1880's.

In truth, the body of the girl was stolen from Kinnettles by a group of young men who were friends of a local medical student. They buried it under the manure pile at the Wellington Hotel Livery and let the manure "do its thing". In August of 1880 they dug up the remains and boiled them in a maple syrup kettle to thoroughly clean the bones. When the medical student returned to university in September he was accompanied by the servant girl, a mere skeleton of her former self! On completion of his schooling he returned to Fergus and set up practise in a small house beside the Wellington Hotel. Of course, he brought his skeleton with him and she continued to haunt the house until it was taken down in the 1970's. The good doctor did not mind her company, but she had a disturbing effect on more recent inhabitants of the house.

If you visit the Fergus Market Building and find yourself talking to a middle-aged man in rough work clothes, do not offer to shake his hand nor look him in the eye. You will reach for thin air and will see great pain in his grey-blue eyes. You have seen the ghost of a worker who was tragically caught in a belt in the woodworking shop at Beatty Bros. and killed. A number of people who worked in the building in the 1940-60's have sworn they saw him.

Should you walk by the apartments at 250 Queen Street East and see a pretty little girl playing on the lawn in a white dress, look again. The dress is c.1910; so is the little girl. The lawn is a parking lot. The girl is the child of an English couple who died of influenza within days of each other, leaving the child parentless. She was bundled up and sent back to Britain, but she died before reaching Montreal. Her parents are buried in Fergus. She is buried in a small Catholic cemetery near Cornwall, Ontario. Her body may be in Eastern Ontario. Her spirit is in Fergus.

Packing chicks at the Tweddle hatchery on St. David Street, c.1950.

If you see a beautiful sheepdog sitting forlornly on the bank of the Grand River in Centennial Park on Queen Street East, do not be concerned if he does not respond to your call. He belonged to Alexander Ferrier and drowned in the river while trying to reach his master on the far side. Loyalty led him onto thin ice at the call of his master. He has been seen on the riverbank for the past one hundred and thirty years.

A book about Fergus would not be complete without telling about the "legacy of the one-legged chickens". During the 1930-40's John C. Tweddle gained a reputation for his chicken hatchery. Eggs were placed in specially built incubators which were electrically controlled. After hatching, the chicks were placed in special boxes and shipped to destinations around North America, indeed around the world after World War II. Only the best chicks were selected for sale. Those eggs which failed to hatch, or chicks which failed the "tests" of two legs, two wings, two eyes etc., were put in a huge metal garbage pail placed at the back of the hatchery for disposal.

People in Fergus tended to have the oddest assortment of chickens in their flock, misshapen, one-legged, blind cacklers who produced eggs as well as the Grade A Tweddle product. They were also tasty in the stew-pot, once fattened up. Fergusites, who had flocks of chickens, regularly checked the garbage pails to see what poor, miserable specimens they could save. Sometimes the heat of the summer hatched some of the eggs put out and perfectly healthy chicks were found.

If J.C. Tweddle knew what was going on he never fussed about it. Granny's flock consisted of any number of sightless, wingless, mottle-feathered friends. We children added to it on a regular basis by dragging home anything that moved in the pails – that no one else had gotten to first.

Fergus: Wet and Dry

Few topics can create such a stir as "drink" can in Fergus, even today. The following stories of yesteryear clearly illuminate the social mores and beliefs prevalent at the time. All of these tales were gleamed from the reminiscences of the author's grandmother, her parents and their friends.

Shortly after the settlement was established, a distillery was erected. It turned out "tolerable" whiskey and its product was well received by settlers and visitors alike. During the first twenty years the community found itself supporting two distilleries and two breweries. Drink was important in a Scotsman's diet. The spirits were not only used for medicinal purposes, but they played a vital role in the social life of the area. Granted, parties tended to get a little rough after an evening with the "cathur", but they would have been much rougher without! Free liquor was what kept men working during a "bee". Liquor was drunk internally and applied externally for human and beast. It was as much a part of a Scotsman's life as breathing.

In the late 1840's a temperance movement took root in Upper Canada. With slogans such as "water not cathur" these brave souls tried to stem the flow of the golden nectar. They had little luck in the Upper Canadian bush.

In 1852, a Temperance Hall was built in Fergus at 420 St. Andrew Street West, but floundered shortly thereafter. No drinker would darken its doors. Male non-drinkers were not fussy about publicly stating their stand. Women, who initially raised the money for the hall, were not wage earners and therefore could not afford the upkeep of the hall. As long as the Fergus breweries and distilleries continued to manufacture their product, they found a ready market in the community.

Temperance Hall, built 1852 at 420 St. Andrew Street West.

By the 1880's the Beatty influence was being felt. One brewery and one distillery closed under some pressure. In the 1870's Fergus could boast eight "wet" hotels, but by the 1890's there were only four in operation, three wet and one nearly bankrupt. The remaining distillery was soon to close. Suddenly one evening the remaining brewery blew up while the Temperance Union Women were at prayer. The minister in charge said it was "an answer from heaven"; the night watchman at the brewery said it was a "malfunction in a gauge" that caused the explosion.

The ruins of the brewery were still to be seen on the hill between St. Patrick and St. George Street in the 1920's (beside the curling club). The remains were taken down when the first arena was built on the site. The beautiful, clear artesian well which supplied the brewery still flows, albeit underground, to the river. Its water bubbles from an underground river which passes across the north end of the village.

During Prohibition, in the 1920's, the "cathur" was available if one knew where to get it. After Prohibition, Fergus remained dry and stayed that way for nearly thirty-five years. The exodus on Saturday nights to Elora, St. Jacobs, Kitchener and Guelph was a sight to behold. People resorted to manufacturing their own wines, with dandelion and elder-berry being the most popular. A sigh of relief was heard around town when its citizens finally voted "wet" again. Recently it was found out that although Fergus voted "dry" in the 1930's the vote was never properly registered. The village could have remained "wet"!

Some great stories are told about the "cathur" and its affects. Some of the most hilarious stories involved James Edwards, "the Major", who was also the local gravedigger. Edwards, like George Clephane, was a remittance man. When he served bar at Hugh Black's tavern one could be assured that there would be a disturbance of some sort. After he had succeeded in getting the young men of the village drunk, Edwards loved to bait them for sport.

He is reputed to have spent as much time in the grave as above it for he invariably fell into the hole he was digging. On one occasion Edwards neglected to dig the hole deep enough to hold the coffin. The box and its contents were left at the side of the grave while James presumably dug a little deeper. Those bearing the coffin (that of an unknown and unfortunate Highlander who died while passing through the village) went off for fortification. When they returned they found the hole deep enough. James sat on the pile of dirt which now covered the coffin, finishing off his latest bottle.

"I canna' bury the man if I canna' find him,' Edwards was reputed to have said. "Ye' took him wi' ye' for a wee wake, dinna' ye?'"

After one particularly "spirited" Irish wake, the coffin and body were left behind at the house, while family and friends proceeded to the graveyard. The mistake was discovered only when the mourners reached the cemetery and they had to go all the way back to retrieve the body, some three miles from home! However, while they were gone a neighbour had noticed the oversight and had loaded the coffin on his sleigh and driven over the fields to the cemetery. When the mourners arrived back at the house, the coffin and body were gone! When the neighbour arrived at the gravesite the mourners were gone! The neighbour lowered the coffin into the grave, threw some dirt over it and left for home where he proceeded to get quite drunk. The mourners walked to Guelph to report a stolen body. It was the next day before they found the body was where it should have been in the first place. By that time everyone was sober enough to understand what had happened.

Another story has "the Major" crawling up Provost Lane one evening on his way home (his cabin was at that time conveniently built by the brewery) when he came head to head with a pig.

"'You be an ugly woman," he said, "but I'm no' fussy.'"

The stories of the Scots and their drink abound. Another Fergus favourite tells of one old Scotsman and his hogshead of beer kept in the basement, just under the kitchen sink. He was a bachelor and a bit eccentric. He installed a small cistern pump on a dry sink and dropped the pipe into the hole in the hogshead, making provision for the barrel to "breath". His beer literally flowed like water, until Dr. Groves had to perform an operation on him on his kitchen table and tried to wash his hands in the man's beer – true suds!

A ceremony which takes place each year at the Tattoo, as part of Fergus Scottish Festival is an adaption of a Celtic "housewarming". The author researched many of the customs of the Scots, Celts and Gaels before she put pen to paper to write *Ingle Kenl't – Hearthflame Rekindled*. Some of the lines are a literal translation of an old Gaelic hearth blessing. The "cathur" played an important part in the ritual of lighting a new hearth and welcoming people to a community. "Cathur" is a lowland Scottish term for liquor – any drinkable alcoholic spirits.

As hot coals are brought to a central hearth from the four compass points...

From the Northern white of the winter's snow,
From the eastern blue of the spring's new moon,
From the southern red of the Autumn's leaves,
From the western gold of the summer's sun,
Come the coals of the hearthflame,
Entrusted to the hands of friends.
Though the fire has died in the olden house,
Its spirit remains alive.
When touched to the wood in the newlain hearth,
The warmth is rekindled again.

For warmth is friendship,
And friendship is love.
And love is bestowed upon all.
Let the door forever be open,
Let the Cathur run free.
It is sung far and wide
That this e're may be.

The home is the hearth.
The hearth is the flame.
The flame is the spirit of love.
Let all know, from whence they came
They have been warmed by this hearth and this flame.

Poetic Expression of the Past

Fergus has had a number a talented individuals in its midst. Some achieved recognition in the area; several others found fame across Canada. One woman, Jane Ann Henderson, went completely unrecognized until well after her death. Even now little is known of her poetry.

Jane Ann arrived in Fergus in November 1911, one year after her husband. She brought two children with her, John age eight and James only four. She had a third son, Walter (Scotty) in 1912. Jane adapted to life in Fergus, but missed her homeland so much that it prompted her to write poems in order to express and release her feelings. Scotty Henderson remembered his mother sitting at the kitchen table writing for hours, but did not realize what she was doing until years later when only seven of her many poems were found. No one knows what happened to the rest of Jane Ann Henderson's writings. A search is underway for any that might have been submitted for publishing under the name Jane Ann or Elizabeth Henderson. Regrettably Jane Ann never did return to Scotland, but we are indebted to her for the most beautiful poem, *Home Longings* and for the poignancy of *A Woman's Question*.

HOME LONGINGS

Sighs my heart, as the winds are sighing,
Roam my thoughts, as the sea birds roam.
Over the wastes of ocean flying,
Sick with longing for the sight of home.

Here afar, as in desert spaces,
Pines my soul in a vain regret.
Oh, for the dear familiar faces,
Oh, for the scenes around them set.

Naught of worth can the wide world offer,
Naught of joy can the sad heart know.
Only the solace of dreams that proffer,
Memories blest of the long ago.[40]

A WOMAN'S QUESTION

Do you know, you have asked, for the costliest thing
Ever made by the hand above.
A woman's heart and a woman's life and a woman's wonderful love.
Do you know you have asked for the priceless thing,
As a child might ask for a toy;
Demanding what others have died to win,
With the reckless dash of a boy.
You have written my lesson of duty out,
Manlike you have questioned me.
Now stand at the bar of my woman's soul
Until I shall question thee.
You require your mutton shall always be hot,
Your socks and your shirt shall be whole.
I require your heart, to be true as God's stars
And pure as heaven your soul.
You require a cook for your mutton and beef.
I require a far better thing;
A seamstress, you're wanting for stocking and shirts,
I look for a man and a king.
A king for a beautiful realm called home.
And a man that the maker, God
Shall look upon as he did the first, and say it is very good.
I am fair and young but the rose will fade,
From my soft young cheek one day;
Will you love me then mid the falling leaves,
As you did in the bloom of May?

Is your heart an ocean so strong and deep,
I may launch all on its tide.
For a loving woman finds heaven or hell,
On the day she becomes a bride.
I require all things that are grand and true,
All things that a man should be;
If you give this all I would stake my life
To be all you demand of me;
If you cannot do this, a laundress and cook
You can hire with little to pay.
But a woman's heart and a woman's love,
Are not to be won that way.[41]

Men must be given their fair share of the poetical stage. A.D. Ferrier, an early settler and chonricler of the past, also wrote some interesting verse. Two of his better known poems are *The Chopper's Song* and *Changed are the Days* both written around 1865.

THE CHOPPER'S SONG

The sun shines bright on the sparkling snow,
The cattle are fed, to the wood we'll go.
We'll lower the pride of yon maple tall
Ere the rays of the sun on the noon-mark fall.

Then away we go with our axes bright,
Which glance in the sun, like the diamond bright.
And soon there is heard 'neath the forest wide,
The sound of the axe as we notch its side.

Such music is sweet to the settler's ear,
As the crack of the axe rings firm and clear,
And the chips fly fast, and the blood runs warm,
As with skillful vigor, we ply the arm.

Stand clear – it goes! No, one more stroke,
And the heart of the noble tree is broke;
With a long, loud groan, and a thundering roar
'Midst the scattering snow lies the monarch hoar.

What a beautiful tree! Almost two feet through.
Hurrah for the men of the axe and plough!
Oh! Give us peace 'neath our own loved Queen,
And we'll soon make the forest a garden, I we'en.[42]

CHANGED ARE THE DAYS

Changed are the days since the cedars dark
Dipped their sprays in the rapid stream,
As it rushed along to the deep, black pool,
Almost hid from the sun's bright beam.

Ah! Gone are the friends of that olden time,
The pioneers bold and true,
Who toiled for their home in the forest wild,
Far away from their mountains blue.

For howl of the wolf is heard no more,
Nor is seen the bounding deer;
Hushed is the cry of the whip-poor-will,
Of the saw-wetter sharp and clear.

All things on this earth with times may change,
And on earth true friends must part;
But a better land and a heavenly home,
Await the true Christian heart.[43]

Meeting of the SRS Club (a sewing club), c.1938, at "Blackburn" on Lamond Street.

Feats of Strength and the Highland Games

Evidence has surfaced in the past year to indicate that Scottish Athletic Events were an important part of a young man's summer life in the settlement. It had been believed that lowland Scottish people paid little attention to those feats of strength which were so dear to the hearts of the Highlanders. However, in letters which were found in 1989 in the Byerly collection, James Webster mentions "throwing the stone" with his good friend, the Provost. He also mentions that the trees were straight enough that "good cabers could be obtained." It is best to let the words of one of the settlers speak for the sport. From the pen of James Perry we find:

Fergus in the old days was renowned for Scottish sports. The MacIntosh boys – John, James and Dougall – from the Highlands were wonderful throwers of the hammer and putters of the shoulder stone. They had keen rivals in Henry Michie, merchant, and the Clarks of Bona Cord (sic).

The hammer was thrown by sheer strength in those days, the thrower standing fast at the scratch. Later on, when the exploits of Roderick Maclennan of Glengarry became known, his wonderful and fearful performance of swinging the hammer round his head and rotating his body three times from a distance of fifteen feet up to the scratch before letting the hammer go, the standfast delivery in Fergus was abandoned and Maclennan's style adopted. We boys commenced to initate the stalwarts in their sports and some of us became quite expert in hammer throwing in Maclennan's way, a style that enabled us easily to increase the throw over one-third the distance of a throw made by standing fast. George Anderson and my cousin, John Watt, were two of the best athletes in the school. Half a dozen of us had many an evening contest on the sloping field behind the auld kirk yard, some of us winning at one time and others at another, as the proper assimilation of our porritch (sic) and bacon gave us strength and elasticity. I often attribute this youthful exercise with the hammer and stone to the lengthened years of some of our lives.

Five years after my school days were over, and after I had quit my youthful athletic sports, I happened to be an attached officer of the 13th Battalion of Hamilton for a short time, and one year atttended a picnic held by the regiment at Queenston Heights. An elaborate programme of sports was prepared for the men – running, wrestling, jumping, stone putting, caber tossing, and throwing the sledge hammer. I watched the big muscular men one after another straining themselves throwing the hammer as far as they could in the old-fashioned way, with a big, circular crowd looking on over a vacant space of about thirty yards in diameter.

Turning to Lieutenant Gwyn, a fellow officer, I said, "Gwyn, I think I can beat those men at the game."

"What you?" he replied. "What do you know about throwing hammers against men double your weight? How much do you weigh?"

"Oh, about a hundred and sixty."

"Ha-ha-ha!" he laughed.

That settled it. I called the man directing the sports and I told him, "I would like to enter the hammer event if not too late." He looked at me with a smile and said, "All right, sir, come along." So, amid much laughter and banter from my fellow officers standing about, I whipped off my sword, belt and tunic and stepped up to the scratch.

Picking up the 12 pound hammer and giving it a whirl, I said to the man in charge: "Please ask the crowd in front yonder to stand back twenty yards." Another grin, and a shout: "Stand back there, you people," waving his arm at the spectators in front. More laughter all round. I then took my position fifteen feet behind the scratch and swung the hammer in my right hand around my head three times, increasing its velocity, rotated my body three times as I whirled to the scratch with my swinging hammer. And when I let it go at the scratch it sailed through the air and landed at the edge of the fleeing crowd, nearly double the distance of the longest throw of a big blacksmith who was counting himself the winner. "Ho! Ho!" "Hurrah! Hurrah!" shouted the crowd in amazement.

The astonished blacksmith came over to me and said: "Let me feel your muscle, sir." I dropped my arm, limp, when he put his brawny fingers on my sleeve. "Good lord," he said, turning to his companions, "and the youngster has no muscle, as far as I can feel."[44]

In the 1890's there was one day set aside each July for Scottish Athletic competition in Fergus. One gentleman from Kincardine took the prize for the caber toss year after year until he eventually moved from the area. The Fergus caber, at that time, always weighed in at approximately 233 lbs!

Fergus Highland Games began in 1946 when a number of individuals, led by Alex F. W. Robertson, approached the newly formed Chamber of Commerce to suggest that they sponsor a Highland Games. Mr. Robertson believed the Scottish heritage of the community was being lost as other nationalities came to populate the area and as the new generations became more removed from their homeland.

The first Highland Games was one of the most traditional, with band and dance competitions, all types of athletic events including

Piper Percy Gibson.

road races, high jump and broad jump along with the traditional hammer throw and caber toss. As it rained (a wee bit) the committee sustained a loss of three-hundred dollars which they covered from their own pockets. To the credit of the Chamber, who saw the economic benefits of such a day, the Highland Games has become a yearly event, always held in August – sometimes on the third Saturday – sometimes on the second Saturday. During the early 1960's the second Saturday in August was selected as the permanent day and Victoria Park declared the permanent home for the event. Under the leadership of a number of capable managers, the Highland Games became one of the best-known in Ontario, and possibly one of the largest.

In the early 1980's it became apparent that the games, in order to retain their status as one of the

Young participants in the 1940s.

Fergus will remember Keith Tice as a keen competitor, a consummate gentleman, and a friend. He died in his 42nd year near Clovis, California.

best, had to improve and expand their activities. The author personally had the pleasure of working for seven years with General Manager, Robert (Bob) Kerr, who through his far-sighted management, brought the festival to a three day happening – Friday evening through Sunday. Another volunteer who did a mammouth amount of work was Percy Gibson, a gentleman and piper of distinction. Under Percy's supervision the Friday night Tattoo, which began in 1988, became one of the best attended and fastest growing events of the festival. Percy could take nine bands who had never played together before they met on the parade field four hours before the Tattoo and "mold" them into a fantastic show that spectators assumed had been rehearsed for weeks. Of course, they did not see what went on behind the scenes as the Tattoo unfolded before them! The most visually spectacular and moving part of the Tattoo was *Ingle Kenl't – Hearthflame Rekindled* which, in a beautiful ceremonial lighting of a hearth, warmly welcomed all visitors to Fergus and beckoned them to stay and enjoy the hospitality of the community.

When activities were expanded to Sunday in 1991, the World Musclepower Championships were staged. This most unique and unu-

Highland Fling competition, Fergus Highland Games, 1988.

Massed bands led by George Forgan, who before his death was President of the Pipers and Pipe Band Society of Ontario.

sual strongman competition had never been held before in North America. In the years following, Sunday became a day devoted to Scottish traditions.

During my eleven-year tenure with the festival, it acquired World Class event status, expanded to three days, received the North American Scottish Heavy Events Championships and the North American Tug-of-War Championship titles, and received international recognition as the festival "on the edge" – the Scottish festival to be watched for innovative yet traditional additions.

In 1992 the name of Fergus Highland Games was officially changed to Fergus Scottish Festival and the event was incorporated. This new name more accurately reflected the weekend of activities. Despite the name change the emphasis of the weekend remains on the Fergus Highland Games which is held on the Saturday of the Fergus Scottish Festival Weekend. Fergus, and in particular Victoria Park, have become known as the "home of the Highland Games".

The fiftieth year of the Fergus Highland Games, in 1995, continues to keep alive the heritage of the Scots who settled the area. The Festival's mission statement is self explanatory:

"Fergus Scottish Festival is dedicated to the preservation of the visual, musical, athletic and written heritage of Scotland." It is hoped that future generations and individuals managing this important event never lose sight of the fact their mandate is to preserve this most unique and fragile heritage. Fragile, because as people do become more removed from their past, they tend to lose interest in the very roots that brought them to this point in their personal historical journey.

It seems appropriate to share a poem written by A. F. W. Robertson, on the occasion of the First Highland Games in 1946:

Oh welcome to Fergus,
Ye bonnie lads and lassies,
Ye pipers and ye dancers
And a' ye Heilin' men
To this our Highland Games Day,
In sich a place sae fair,
A Heilin' welcome ye will get,
Of which here come some makr

There'll be pipin', aye and dancin',
The like ye never seen,
The caber and the hammer
And of course, the Heilin' fling;
Jig and reels and burly chiels,
That will fairly mak' a clamor'
So come awa' ye Scottish Clans,
Ye'll nae hae time to wanner.

This place o' Scottish heritage
Will surely mak' ye cherrie;
So don't forget, ye bonnie lads,
To bring yer ain wee dearie
To this our Highland Games, man,
She'll nae hae time to wearly,
But if by chance she like to dance,
We surely can obledge thee

Come ane, come a', ye big and braw,
A welcome waits ye here,
To this fair place called Fergus,
The place we lo'w sae dear,
To enjoy the Highland Games, Freen,s,
Oh, what a bonnie sicht,
That will live in a' yer mem'ries
For mony a day and nicht.[45]

A Potpourri of Fergus Facts

Sometimes little bits of information come along that in themselves do not make a story, but together make for excellent reading. From the scores of letters, dozens of journals, booklets and books written about the community, and from early copies of the *Fergus News Record* come a collection of happenings and lore on Fergus.

• The first white man to see the Grand River at Fergus may have been Étienne Brûlé (1591-1633) but it is documented that Reverend Father Joseph de La Roche D'Aillon came through in 1626-1627. Perhaps both were beaten out by Samuel de Champlain, who traversed to Georgian Bay in the mid-sixteen hundreds.

• The Grand River was known by many names – Tinaaouta, Rivière Rapide, D'Urfe or Urse, La Rivière D'Urse, Ouse and Grand. Early maps refer to the river in the Fergus area as the Grand River Ouse.[46]

• The Pig Bridge was one of the oddities of Fergus in the 1830's and '40's. Along the river bank, behind today's library, stood a distillery, a granary, a sawmill, a grist mill and a pig shed. The only pasture for these porkers was on the south bank of the river, today known as the Fergus Market parking lot. So that the pigs might get back and forth, a pig bridge was built across the narrowest part of the river. It was a flimsy affair of wood and wire. People whose homes were on the south side of the river soon began to risk the pig bridge to get from the north to the south side. The pig bridge, for one not accustomed to crossing it, was a risky business, especially if one met a pig coming the other way. Eventually the "one span" wooden bridge became two – one for the pigs and one for pedestrians. The only problem was that pigs wouldn't learn which was their half of the bridge. The pig bridge was dismantled when a drunken fellow fell to his death after an encounter with a particularly vicious sow.

• Dr. P.B. Henderson was the first physician in Fergus. He arrived in 1835 and left during the same year.

• December 1835 was very cold with snow three to four feet deep and temperatures hovering around thirty below zero Fahrenheit. Travel was almost impossible and many settlers suffered from cabin fever.

• Mrs. T.V. Johnston was the first Presbyterian to have a grave-side burial service in Fergus. Graveside services were not encouraged as ministers felt the church the most suitable place to say good-bye.

• Webster's bachelor hall was known as "The Cleihum", the gathering place, and was located at 201 St. Andrew Street West.

• Settlers continued the practise of naming their homes and estates as they had in Scotland. Some of the more familiar in Fergus were: Myrtlebank, the home of Henry Michie on Gowrie Street and former home of James Webster; Hermitage Hill, the home of James Dick in West Garafraxa; Maple Leaf Farm, the home of William Louttit in West Garafraxa; Rosecrea, the home of Mr. & Mrs. John Anderson; Fairfield, the home of Jacob Dix of West Garafraxa; Ravenswood, the home of John H. Broadfoot in Nichol Township; Lyle Hill, the home of Robert Brooks on Hill Street; Hazelhurst, the home of James Russell on St. David St. South; Briarlea located at 525 Union Street East; Parkview Cottage, 165 Union Street West; Ingleside, 149 Garafraxa Street East; Collar Green, 200 Union Street East; Glencourse, 180 Queen Street East – known later as Grovehurst, the home of Dr. Groves; Royal Oak Farm, the home of Wilson Ramson; Drumness, the home of John Ewen, Nichol Township; Bagley House, known later as Stonehome, the home of Clara and Georgina Young.

• Letters not called for at the Fergus Post Office in September of 1847 included ones for Elizabeth Barker, Adam Brown, Alex Clark, Alex Cormie, Robert Dawson, Duncan McCuag, Nicholas Murphy, Robert Morrison, John Munro, Adam Stewart, Alex Shearer, Robert Whiltson and James Wilson. Considering the fact that one had to pay the postage on the letter, it might be weeks before the receiver would pick up the mail. It was advertised who had letters so that if necessary, friends and relatives could help pay the postage.

• Absalom Shade, an American and brother-in-law of Alexander Harvey of Kinnettles took it into his head to get some good axes made in Scotland. He made a nice model in wood, but neglected to put an eye in it for the handle. The model was sent to Scotland and in due course one hundred fine axes were sent to Fergus – none with an eye for the handle. They were useless as axes but Shade, always the businessman sold them as doorstops. They became known as Shades Wedges.

• Native Indians continued to traverse the area around Fergus until the 1850's, camping in the Beaver Meadow above Garafraxa Street West which is now a housing development.

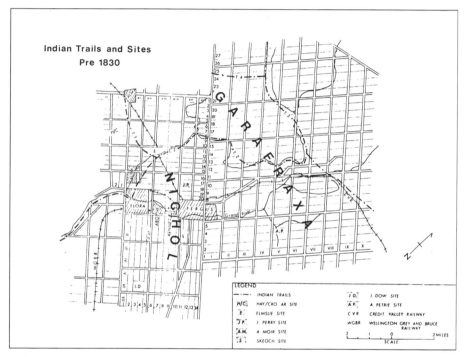

Indian trails.

• In 1850 James Webster built a double span, wooden bridge over the river at St. David Street, so he could drive to his mansion on Gowrie Street without taking the long route over the Tower Street bridge. This bridge consisted of a centre pier of timber weighed down with stones. It was constantly in need of repair. By 1876 the bridge was badly in need of extensive rebuilding and a wooden bridge with stone abutments was built. This bridge was partially paid for by the County and partially by town residents.

• The year 1854 must have had an extra day in it for there is a man buried in the Auld Kirk Yaird by the name of Robt. McGillvray who died on February 30, 1854 at age 41. He is listed as a native of Nairnshire, Scotland. As no records of this man can be found, it is thought he was a displaced Highlander passing through Fergus. Someone purchased a tombstone for him. But why the unusual date?

• In 1855 John Campbell Ross Jr. came to stay with A.D. Ferrier in Fergus. The house located at 230 Hillside Drive was home to his father, mother, six brothers and two sisters before they managed to find good farmland in West Garafraxa. John Campbell Ross Jr. left a written legacy for Fergus. His diary jottings are marvellous and picturesque. He mentions highly respected Presbyterian pigs, who at the prompting of a prankster, walked quietly down the aisle of the Free Church.[47]

• In 1857, A.D. Ferrier became the first president of the Horticultural Society. An Agricultural Society was formed in 1835.

• Fergus became a village on January 1, 1858; and a town in 1953. When Fergus officially became a village some people railed against the move toward progress. Quotes in the paper ranted, "We'll have 2,000 people living here before you know it". If they could see Fergus now!

• Ann Inglis, was not only one of the women who had "Buist's vote", she was also the first woman to own land in Fergus. She was given a village lot when Webster married.

• In 1858 the village advertised for a Bell Ringer. The bell was to be rung four times a day, Sundays excepted. No one dared work on Sunday in a Presbyterian village, not even the Bell Ringer. The salary was not to exceed $4.00 per month. William Ralph was appointed as Bell Ringer and was instructed he must keep railway time and the bell was to be rung as punctually as possible. The times for the bell were 6:00 a.m., 12:00 noon, 2:00 p.m. and 6:00 p.m. John Gerrie became the last Bell Ringer in Fergus when he ended his job on October 24, 1912. At eight-three years of age, Mr. Gerrie, no longer felt equal to the task of constantly ringing the bell every winter's day. Besides, it meant walking up the fifty-six steps to reach the rope. The bell was located in the tower of the old Town Hall/Council Chamber on the north corner of Tower and St. Patrick Streets.

• Not only was there the Beatty whistle that regulated everyone's lives, the Broomfield Mills had a whistle they blew every day. Monkland Mills had an alarm which they blew for a fire. Abraham Groves Electric Light Plant had an unpredictable whistle and a siren that went off at all times during the day or night. When all four blew simultaneously the sound was unbelievable!

- In August of 1861, John Watt and sixty-two other citizens petitioned council not to have the large stone removed from James Square. The granite stone remains today with the holes drilled in it to hold the explosives. That is how close it came to be blown out of the square and out of town history. This is the famous "Kissing Stone" of Fergus.

- In December of 1868 the new Fergus Drill Shed and Town Hall was officially opened. In 1985 this building came down amid protests of a large number of residents. It, unfortunately became the scapegoat for two feuding church groups, the United Church fighting – again!

- In 1868 a new stagecoach going directly to Guelph was started by John Gerrie of the St. Andrew's Hotel. The St. Andrew's Hotel which stood on the west corner of Tower and Queen streets is now a private residence.

- In 1870 the following buildings were erected in Fergus: a new sewing machine factory, a shingle factory, a brewery, two hotels and forty new homes. Henry Michie built a new mansion on Gowrie Street on the former Webster estate. A. Anderson built the Royal Hotel on the west corner of Provost and St. Andrew Street.; G.D. Fergusson built ten "Balloon" cottages on Hill and St. George Streets to house various workmen attracted to the community by the increase in job opportunities. Most of these workmen were of Irish heritage.

- The first bankrobbery in Fergus took place in 1873 when the Bank of Montreal was robbed of some silver and valuables stored for safekeeping. One item taken was an old gold watch of unusual shape that belonged to Adam Fergusson.

- The village jail used to be located in the partial basement of the Town Hall, which stood to the west of Melville United Church, now a parking lot. When the jailer had special prisoners, those that were being transferred from one jail to another, he used to take them home to stay overnight. He was ashamed of the jail cell he had to offer. More than one time his wife cooked a hearty meal for a robber. Once she played hostess to a murderer.

- The job of constable in the village was an interesting one. For the year 1874 the constable's duties included the following: attend all professional business; take charge of the drill shed, fireman's hall and engine house; see that the fire engine is at all time in thorough working order and care for all apparatus, clothing and property belonging to the fire brigade; take charge and look after all corporation tools and implements;

Mario Landoni Senior, c.1919, police constable and chief.

prepare and cut the wood required in the drill shed, firemen's hall and engine house; repair all sidewalks, clean and look after ditches and work upon the streets when required; take care of Belsyde Cemetery and keep it in order as may be directed by the cemetery committee; collect the young men's tax and perform such other duties as the council may from time to time direct.[48]

• In 1874 a bridge across the Grand River at Johnston Street was condemned for traffic. This bridge was wooden and was at one time on the main road between Fergus and Elora. Before the Poor House was built on the upper road, now County Road #18, the road between the two communities lay on the south side of the river.

• For the Christmas of 1877 the sixteen pupils of St. Joseph's Catholic School presented their teacher, John Shea, with a writing desk. To get to school some of these students had to walk three miles there and back every day.

• On November 22, 1878, the new high school,which stood beside St. Andrews Presbyterian Church and which was torn down in the 1940's, was opened by the Honourable Adam Clark and Professor Goldwyn Smith. Thomas Young did the masonry work and Robert H. Couse did the carpentry work.

• In February of 1879 Constable J. Alpaugh was hired for $1.00 per day, Sunday included. By September of 1880 he was allowed to purchase a dark lantern, a baton, a pair of nippers and a belt. In September of 1882 the constable was given a raise of $0.10 per day. In November of 1884, exasperated by the new duty of lighting the street lamps, Constable Alpaugh asked for more money. He was refused on the grounds that the lamps required little more than an hour of his attention each night.

• In 1880 people in Fergus saw their first electric light display when a circus came through the village with a display and demonstration. Dr. Abraham Groves paid particular attention to this display! He would, in a few years, introduce electric light to Fergus and Elora.

• Between 1880 and 1895 over three thousand trees: spruce, pine and maple were planted in the village. These trees were placed on both public and private lands in an attempt to replace those lost to development of the community. So many trees had been cut by the early settlers that the village was bare of all original forestation, with the exception of three tall elm trees that somehow missed the axe. The need to replant trees is most apparent in the 1990's with many of the originals dying from various air pollutants and land development.

• Each year, usually in April, civic-minded citizens converged on Victoria Park for a "rock party". They picked stones off the grass in preparation for the outdoor lacrosse season. The site of Victoria Park was originally a swamp which was land filled with rock and rubble so that a race course could be built on the site.

• A Scot who went to the Free Church, and not having any coinage, placed a bill on the plate. He expected change but didn't get any. Consequently he instructed his wife not to pay the minister for his burial, should he die before her. He left all his money to the Catholic Church, except that which he left her to live on.

• An original by-law of the Fire Brigade prohibited the use of tobacco at their meetings. Nothing was said about liquor.

• Sir Lyman Duff, who was born at Speedside just south of Fergus, started as a law student in the office of N.L. Munro in Fergus in the early 1880's.

• Dr. William Mutch was the first person to own a piano in Fergus. Mrs. James Campbell Ross was the second. They acquired their piano's c.1881 from J & R Craig, St. Andrew Street West, Fergus.

• Trees were planted in James Square in May of 1883. Some people objected saying the view of St. Andrews Presbyterian Church would be blocked. The comment from tree supporters was that in fifty years time those complaining wouldn't be around to see the view anyway.

• The telephone came to Fergus in 1886. The exchange was located at the back of "Goldsmith Hall", a jewellery store owned by Samuel Marshall at 109 St. Andrew Street West. The first telephone directory of that year listed twelve subscribers: Black, John, Elevator; Black, John, Office; Black, John, Residence; Canadian Pacific R'y Station; Draine, John L., Hardware Merchant; Grand Trunk R'y Station; Dr. A. Groves, Office; Imperial Bank; Marshall, S., Jeweller, Goldsmith's Hall; Marshall, S., Residence; O'Reilly, Dr. Gerald, Office; Wilson, James, Monkland Flour and Oatmeal Mills.

Men viewed the box with trepidation and when forced to answer would gingerly pick up the receiver and shout into the mouthpiece as though they were calling the cows in from the back forty. Some men refused to answer the contraption. " Get the phone, Maggie," Munro used to call everytime he heard it ring. Womenfolk knew the telephone to be the greatest invention since packaged yeast. If you wished the village to know about a wedding, death, birth you simply picked up the receiver. Dr. Groves had one of the first telephones in the village. He used to order everyone off the line before he spoke. If he suspected old Grandma Morrow was still listening he would whisper. Invariably she would say "speak up, speak up. I can't hear you" and she would be caught! In exasperation Groves once announced that she had died the evening before, poor soul. "I did not!" she retorted. Caught again.[49]

• In 1888 at the 24th of May celebrations a lacrosse ball was thrown a record distance of 465 feet by John Black. J.M. McKenzie Watt promptly also threw one 456 feet. The previous record was 422 feet set by a Montreal man.

Bell Switchboard Operators Ann Fenwick and Pearl Munn, 1937, in the old Bell Telephone Building on St. Andrew Street.

- In 1888 in six weeks Robert Craig sold 26 organs, 6 pianos and 32 sewing machines in Fergus.

- In August 1888, at a meeting of the Country Bridge Committee, it was decided to build a steel bridge across the River on Tower Street to replace the wooden structure. The contract was let to the Kincardine Bridge Company at $1,125.00 and the bridge was seventy-two feet long by twenty feet wide. The bridge opened December 6th, 1888. In 1910, this bridge in turn was replaced by the first concrete bridge to span the Grand River.

- Dr. G.A. Reid's house became the first in Fergus to be heated with hot water c.1892, although he had hot water in his surgery in 1884.

- In February 1893 Pauline Johnson, the famous Indian poet from "Chiefswood" near Brantford, gave a concert and reading in the Town Hall. When she stood on stage in native regalia there was such a silence in the hall that she could hear the pocket watches of the men in attendance.

- Twice in 1896 Wyllie's Distillery in Fergus was seized by the officers of the law on charges of revenue fraud.

- In May of 1897 four hundred and thirty trees were planted on the high ground on the south eastern and north portions of Victoria Park and around the outside park fence. At the same time a fine grandstand was erected to accommodate three hundred and forty people with five refreshment booths below, all partitioned off and floored. The grandstand came down in the late 1950's, but many of the trees still stand.

- The second murder in the history of Fergus and area was in the early 1900's when the body of a baby was found on the ice below the Tower Street Bridge. It was thought the baby was born sometime during the night to a woman passing through the community and was thrown over the bridge.

- In the early 1900's members of the Free Church simply walked away from their building, leaving personal bibles, communion set and church bible behind. This time the dispute had fractured the congregation for good. The Free Church building was purchased by Charlie Mattaini who used it for a stable before restructing the building into a house. Charlie sold the building to the Craig family whose members lived there until the 1980's. The building still stands behind the tennis courts on Union Street West.

- In February of 1901 Jimmie Forrester of Fergus defeated John

Nelson, Champion Fast Skater of the World by ten yards in a magnificent exhibition of speed skating. In January 1901 there was a one mile skating race between Jack Curtis and William Thomson at the Fergus rink, the wood structure on Tower Street South, east corner of Albert and Tower Streets. Contestants had to remember to stay well to the inside of the track and keep their heads low as the sloping sides of the tin building were hazardous to one's health.

• In May of 1901 over one hundred people attended a reunion for students of the old log school. The log school stood on the site of James MacQueen Public School on St. George Street.

• In 1906 a gravestone was purchased by public subscription and erected in Belsyde cemetery to the memory of A.D. Ferrier who donated land to be used for a new cemetery in the 1860's. In 1876 trees were planted on both sides of Princess Street leading to the cemetery by A. Cadenhead. Cadenhead was paid $44.75 for the job. In 1882 the cemetery had been fenced and 200 spruce and 200 hardwood trees were planted in the unused portions of the grounds.

• When a horse strayed onto the tracks of the CNR in June of 1906, two engines and thirteen freight cars ran off the track above the Allardice school causing a spectacular accident.

• In June of 1906 the 105 foot stack for the electric light plant was finished. It was built by Charlie Mattaini's construction crew and contained 45,000 bricks and fifteen cords of stone. The chimney had a thirty-eight inch square flue all the way through. In the summer of 1928 the same chimney was dynamited by Charlie as it was no longer needed to generate electric power. Charlie refused to have anyone else destroy his handiwork. He was an expert with explosives and, as his wife used to say, could blow a flea off an elephant's back without the elephant feeling a thing. The bricks were bought by Frank Miller who used them to construct homes on St. George Street East, and St. Andrew Street East.

• The first strike in Fergus was in 1906 when Charlie Mattaini's gang of workmen went out in June for an increase in pay.

• James Beattie, a Fergus resident died on the Titanic in 1913. His body was eventually recovered. His watch that was found on the body, is now in Wellington County Museum and Archives, Fergus.

• J.D. McDonald was the first man to enlist in World War I from Fergus.

• In October of 1914 Grandma Foote (one hundred years old) turned

Cars line St. Andrew Street in this view of the Orange Parade in the 1920s. The Post Office and the American Hotel are prominent buildings.

on the Ontario Hydro Electric power for Fergus. She had celebrated her 100th birthday in May. She could remember Little Falls in the 1830's and viewed electricity as a godsend for everyone.

• Mr. Lanktree owned one of the earlier cars in the village. He lived in a frame house where the parking lot for the Fergus market is now. The make of Mr. Lanktree's car is a source of mystery to even his family although we do know that the car had a two cylinder motor under the seat and was a side crank. There are two schools of thought on this. Mr. Lanktree had a friend in Mount Forest who built himself a car and it could be one of his inventions; on the other hand it could have been an early McLaughlin. Mr. Lanktree was a blacksmith and may have manufactured some of the car parts himself. The article in the *Fergus Elora News Express* (Centennial 1933) did not mention the make of the car. In an old photograph, the car appeared to be a homemade creation. The family still had the photograph in 1983, but unfortunately it has since been misplaced.

HIGHSCHOOL TEACHERS OLD BOYS & GIRLS REUNION (and Pupils) FERGUS CENTENNIAL AUG. 5-9 1933

High School Reunion, 1933.

• In August of 1917 everyone became "Catholic" as no beef was served on Fridays and no bacon any day except for breakfast. This change of diet was to help the war effort.

• In 1919 the firehall was painted for the first time in its fifty-eight year history for a cost of $64.00. This building still stands on the north corner of St. Patrick and Tower Streets and is also known as the Council Chamber. In March of 1872, $2.00 was paid for heating and lighting the Council Chambers four times. The council met in the building monthly.

• During the Second World War, Beatty Bros. Limited had over 1,400 people on their payroll, twelve-hundred of them being munitions workers in the factory. In 1989 a fiftieth anniversary reunion was held with over 650 war workers in attendance. Over two hundred and eighty names were inscribed in an "In Memoriam" book. The author had the pleasure of attending this dinner with her mother, Edith Scott Mattaini.

• In April 1926 the Basket Factory, which is now the site of the Royal Canadian Legion, had eighty young women on its payroll and more were required at times to keep up with the demand for fruit baskets.

• The first aeroplane landed in Fergus during the centennial of its founding in 1933.

• In November, 1939 the Citizens Band of Fergus provided a one-hour long live radio program at a Kitchener radio station .

- The Highland Games were established in Fergus during the same year the Chamber of Commerce was formed, in 1946.
- In March 1947 a snow plow with five engines behind it was buried under the snow on the outskirts of Fergus behind the current L & M Plaza. It took seventy men and another five locomotives to clear the cut, digging through an 18 foot high drift, 160 feet long.
- Once a month the Fergus High School gym and auditorium resounded to the sounds of the big bands and Rock 'n Roll. Teen Town arrived with a bang in the 1950's much to the horror of some of the older teachers. What was worse? Young people in "a hot clutch" or music loud enough to deafen one; and those lyrics! One particular funny sight was Miss Jane Craig trying to do the twist in the teacher's room while the students "burned" the dance floor across the hall. Fifteen cents would buy a bottled cold drink and a doughnut at intermission. Halls were patrolled by lightfooted teachers who coughed a lot as they neared corners. Archie Anderson, the high school custodian, used to "rent" the boiler room to those young adults who wanted to have some privacy. The cost of "rent" was one bottle of orange crush. The same "rent" would get you a hideaway for one period during school hours too. Never fear, parents, Archie did not allow any nonsense in his boiler room. Young people actually did talk. Who can remember being proposed to in the boiler room at the High School? Who can remember sneaking a smoke in the boiler room? Who remembers those teachers who also sneaked a smoke in the boiler room?
- The last gypsy caravan came through Fergus in 1952.
- In November of 1957 the colours of the 153 Battalion were restored and rededicated in St. Andrews Presbyterian Church. The colours had originally been placed in the church in April 1917. The ladies of the church at that time provided a banquet at noon for all attending. A farewell dinner for the troops was given in the Town Hall the same month, with guests and regimental members numbering four hundred and twenty-three. The regiment was under the command of Lt. Col. Thomas Pritchard.

Fergus: My Home

Fergus has always been my home. It was therefore easy to develop an enthusiasm for its written and oral history. I have lived among people who were genuinely interested in the community, its past and its future.

My childhood home is at the foot of the Tower Street Hill, overlooking Victoria Park. The house is a nondescript board and batten structure which belonged to my great grandparents (505 Tower Street South). Grandmother Mattaini lived next door (525 Tower Street South). The unassuming appearance of my family home belied the activity that went on inside. Mother, Edith Scott Mattaini, a woman of immeasurable patience and a great sense of humour, managed to maintain a form of order amidst the chaos of living with an Italian husband who was quick of temper, impulsive in nature and wonderful to have as a father. He was a man with four daughters and a strong-willed mother. Add an eccentric assortment of father's friends, relatives and neighbours (I am not implying our neighbours were eccentric!); two dogs, nineteen cats, three rabbits, a squirrel, a pigeon and you have a stimulating environment, to put it mildly! The animal count decreased and increased with the seasons, as the townspeople knew where to leave unwanted animals. Dad would not let any animal suffer from cold or go hungry.

Granny's house was no haven for rest either. Her door, as ours, was always open. She operated a boarding house and tourist home to supplement her income. After the Second World War there were a large number of displaced Europeans who stayed with her. Count and commoner shared her table. The problems of the world were solved at both dining room tables. Arguments and heated discussions were exciting for a small child, if understood; terribly boring if not.

My favourite quiet spot was a pink granite rock in an overgrown corner of a rail fence on Vinegar Hill. We were never given boundaries and never questioned as to where we could go except for two places, "The Foxhole" and the "Swing Bridge". To get to my rock I had to pass "The Foxhole", a deep and narrow hole at the end of Prince's Street. Limestone bedrock is close to the surface on the south side of the village and water from hills and fields flowed into this hole in the earth. Dad told me the hole was the entrance to a large crevice beneath the surface. He believed that the water flowed into the crevice and then into an underground river, at least three hundred feet below. He didn't discount the fact there were caverns beneath the surface too.

Dad had been told by an "old timer" that the underground river flowed to the north of the village, crossing beneath the Grand River at Kinnettles. Whatever the case, "The Foxhole" absorbed great quantities of field run-off in short periods of time. Once dye was put down the hole so that authorities could ascertain where the water emerged into the Grand River. The dye never showed up in the river. I was warned never to go near the entrance, which was large enough to admit a small dog. Grandmother told me of another "Foxhole" between Fergus and Elora on the south river road that I was equally to avoid.

I shared my granite perch with my best friend, a dog of mixed breed named Pluto. From this vantage point the village lay before me, its moods changing with the seasons. Granny affectionately called Fergus "the Jewel on the Grand", although there were times when she admitted it was a tarnished jewel – in an expensive setting.

The Norman towers on Melville United Church, the Drill Shed and St. Joseph's Church poked through the trees. The spire on St. Andrews Presbyterian Church dwarfed all three as that edifice stood on the highest point of land in Fergus proper; Vinegar Hill was not really in Fergus.

St. Joseph's Catholic church had had a tower as tall and slender as St. Andrews, but one November night in the early 1900's a violent windstorm blew across Ontario. Not only did it sink ships on all the Great Lakes, but it toppled the tower from the Catholic church. The huge ornamental cross embedded itself in St. Patrick Street. Local Orangemen claimed it was "a sign for their cause". Staunch Presbyterians considered it appropriate as they felt the spire far too high. United Church members snickered as they had no tower or steeple to blow down. Catholic parishioners decided to be less conspicuous and capped what was left of the tower.

St. Joseph's sat prominently on its own hill between St. George and St. Patrick Streets. A cemetery shared the hill. When a dump and gravel pit began operations directly west of the cemetery, the burial ground was closed. Catholic Fergusites who died were then buried in Elora, the only "consecrated ground" in the area. Those who opted for burial of their loved ones in Guelph had no love for Elora. Those Catholics that requested their loved ones be buried in Belsyde in Fergus were politely refused until the early 1950's. When Dad was buried in Belsyde Cemetery, people asked what mother had to do or pay, to have a Catholic buried there. Mother was furious!

It is said that when the Lord made the banks of the Gorge just a little bit higher in Elora, he created the rivalry between Fergus and Elora. However, the truth is that the disagreements began in the 1840's when James Webster won an election against Charles Allan. When Allan lost he moved to Elora, three miles down river, taking some of his supporters with him. Whatever the true cause, the two communities never did see eye to eye on anything much again.

One small slight would lead to another. Games of curling and lacrosse were well attended by both sides with insults hurled as fast as stones and balls. When Fergus built a post office, Elora put one up with a higher tower. Elora built a town hall/drill shed; Fergus built a larger one. If

The County House of Industry is today home to the Wellington County Museum and Archives. (Wellington County Museum and Archives)

Fergus had a fire, Elora would have one far more spectacular, even if it meant setting it deliberately. When Elora held a parade, Fergus made sure theirs was longer and larger.

In the 1960's it was decided that the "hatchet" had to be buried once and for all. A party for both communities was planned for the grounds of the Poor House, now the Wellington County Musuem, located midway between the two communities. This site was chosen so that each community had to walk an equal distance. In reality Fergusites made Eloranians walk one-eighth of a mile further. A gold-coloured hatchet was placed in a small "coffin" and buried in a flowerbed on the grounds of the county building. All official pomp and ceremony was used to mark such an auspicious occasion. Children's games were played, cake was served and everyone went home. Before nightfall the hatchet was dug up – so Elora would not steal it, of course! I understand a group from Fergus moved in after dark to steal the "coffin", just before the group from Elora arrived. So much for "burying the hatchet". Of course, today relations between the two communities are much improved, ah hum....

My first year of schooling was in a one-room red brick building located on Catholic church property. In subsequent years my education was obtained in a new two-roomed school fifty yards from the original building. One of our jobs each spring (after a winter of tobogganing and sleighing down the church hill) was to scour the area for all the fragments of bone, teeth and coffin exposed during the winter. The fragments were gathered together and given a decent reburial by our teachers, the Sisters of Notre Dame. At my tender age, it bothered me that Mrs. So & So's tooth was buried with a piece of Mr. So & So's foot. I thought it amounted to adultery. In jest I now like to think our spring ritual was the Sister's own version of May Day celebrations. Instead of planting trees, we planted ancestors, literally.

The commercial area of Fergus ran parallel to the river. The river's course was delineated by the green line of cedar trees growing along both banks. The gorge divided Fergus into two distinct areas – north and south. Many visitors did not, and to this day do not know that the famous "Elora" Grand River Gorge begins in Fergus at Scotland Street, with the prettiest part of the Upper Gorge beginning above the Whirlpool and Mirror Basin just behind the Fergus Market Building.

The morning sun shone on roofs and facades of buildings on the north side of the river. The afternoon sun warmed those on the south side. The north hill claimed Beatty Bros., all the churches (by 1900), the primary school and two-thirds of the population. The South side knew they were from the right-side of the railway track, because the north had all the railway track which ran through Fergus. The north side had all the noise and dirt caused by the trains. We, on the south, heard only the train's whistle as it echoed across the valley. We also boasted of having the high school, Victoria Park and, if you lived on the most prestigious street in Fergus, Union Street, you were known as being a real "Somebody" in the community.

As a child living in a rural agricultural area, horse-drawn farm wagons were still a common sight. I well remember runaway teams racing down St. Andrew Street and brave men leaping to stop them. Once I was thrown against a store window by a man because I was directly in the path of a wild-eyed team of black horses and a thundering farm wagon. At that time Fergus had three feed and chop mills so there was always a steady flow of farm vehicles on the South River Road and Tower Street. The sound of wagons and motorized vehicles mingled with other evidence of life in the valley. These sounds seemed to amplify before they reached Vinegar Hill and my favourite pink granite rock.

Fergus in the 1940's was regulated by whistles and bells. At noon hour the first sound heard was the dull, deep chime of the tower clock at the Post Office. It never completed its twelve laborious gongs before the Beatty steam whistle cut the air with its shrill blast. To the west, on the north side of the river, the melodic tones of the Poor House Bell echoed across the fields, calling the residents to their noon meal.

Just below my rock on the South River Road, the 1840's Free Church Manse, a solid Georgian-style house, sat amidst a smattering of ancient apple and pear trees. Beside it the Mackenzie Watt house brooded in a cover of pine and maple. The Watt house had a secret passage from one bedroom to another, old steamer trunks full of Victorian clothing to try on and great gingerbread cookies dispensed by the reclusive mistress of the house.

At the foot of the hill, a tiny rubblestone cottage hugged the river bank. "Craigshead" was the first stone dwelling built in the settlement about 1836. It was home to the Hugh Black family of fifteen – the same Hugh Black who ran the tavern. Black built a tunnel under the road so his family and livestock would be able to walk from the house to the barn without crossing the busy thoroughfare. Part of that tunnel was a limestone cave. The remains were visible by the roadside, but no one could walk completely through it as most of the tunnel had collapsed during road reconstruction in the early 1920's

The foundations of a vehicular bridge were in Hugh Black's backyard. When the first wooden bridge was swept away by a flood, there were no plans to erect another. But in the early 1900's the foundations of the old bridge were used to anchor a flimsy wood and wire swinging bridge across the river. This was used primarily by workmen travelling from the south side of the village to Beatty Bros. and the Basket Factory on the north side. I was instructed never to cross the swinging bridge, even though my father owned property on the north bank between the bridge and the Basket Factory.

This northside property was originally a limestone quarry and belonged to his father, Charlie Mattaini. During the Second World War Dad drew loam from various sources to make a Victory garden where he grew potatoes in the thin overlay. After the war Dad searched abandoned homesteads for specimens of lilac, honeysuckle, day lily, orange blossom and wild rose. He planted scores of cuttings, rootings and seedlings and turned the upper quarry into a beautiful wild garden he affectionately called "Tangled Garden". He envisioned this garden being the showplace of the community and sold the property to the town fathers in the 1960's with the stipulation it be left as parkland. He sold it for the same amount he had paid in taxes during the years he owned it. It is unfortunate the property did not remain in the hands of the family who would have respected his "Tangled Garden". Unfortunately the park has yet to materialize. In May the lilacs are spectacular. If a breeze blows from the west one can smell lilacs for several blocks.

For a small child, the lure to explore "Tangled Garden" was overwhelming, but I never disobeyed my parents to cross the swinging bridge to get to it. Like myself, all Fergus children had a genuine fear of that bridge. After a man fell to his death from it, the structure was taken down.

The Gow Limestone Quarry was just upriver from "Craigshead". Few people paid attention to the grey-brown rock of the valley bared for all to see. Gow's Quarry was located opposite the Mattaini Quarry and, although not used in the 1950's, still possessed one of its lime burning towers and lots of rusting pieces of equipment. The most interesting was a large steam shovel which had been abandoned where it last worked. In its heyday Gow's Quarry was the largest operation in Wellington County, but by the mid-1950's it had ceased operation.

One summer two geologists stayed with my grandmother while they explored both quarries for sea fossils. As it turned out, a number of rare specimens were found and removed. These fossils are now part of the collection of the Royal Ontario Museum.

When the quarry was operational, fires were kept burning in the kilns day and night. The acrid smell of burning lime hung over the valley when the air was heavy with moisture. When my Uncle Carl was three years old he wandered away from home and somehow climbed the draw slope to the top of the working kiln. His life was saved by a workman who grabbed his legs as he was falling in, head first!

A fascinating story revolved around a house located one block from the quarry on the south corner of Tower and Queen Streets. A Mr. James Campbell built the imposing two and one-half storey wooden house in the late 1840's, during the 1940's it belonged to my grandmother who rented it to several older widows. One day a man, identifying himself as a great grandson of Mr. Campbell, arrived at Granny's door. He asked permission to explore the house. He explained he had letters, testimonials and advertisements indicating that his great grandfather had perfected a remedy for cancer. It seemed that Campbell had concocted a remedy that, if taken internally, worked effectively against the dread disease. He said that people came from far and wide to purchase the medicine. This fellow had all the background information, except for the formula. Immediately he and my Grandmother went to the house. While they were inside looking for the formula, one of the elderly residents remembered she had seen scribbling on the wall in the attic. She admitted she had painted over it because she had wanted a clean looking storage room. When in the attic she could not remember exactly where on the wall the scribbling had been. Unfortunately the boards were rough-cut and no amount of scrapping could remove the battleship grey she had liberally applied. The woman remembered that burdock was one of the words. To this day the "cure" for cancer might lay under the layers of paint in that attic.

Reginald Aubrey Fessenden, the eldest son of an Anglican minister, lived in Fergus briefly between 1872 and 1878. His mother was the founder of the I.O.D.E. – the Imperial Order of the Daughters of the Empire. His childhood home was just a stone's throw away from the

Campbell residence, but on the north side of the river. Reginald Fessenden is famous for such inventions as microphotography, wireless transmission, the first transmission of a human voice by electromagnetic waves – (December 23rd, 1900), as well as the first radio broadcast in the world, made by himself on Christmas Eve, 1906. It consisted of seasonal music and readings. He also "bounced signals off icebergs by radio", measuring the distance in 1913 (the forerunner of radar) and invented the fathometer. One of his most unusual inventions was the transmission of a picture. Could this have been the beginning of television?

Reginald Fessenden.

Fessenden conducted one of his earliest experiments in Fergus. He kept snowballs under leaves in the back of the "CPR" cave, located beside the manse. He caused a major disturbance by throwing them at his father's visitors – in June. Fessemden died on July 22, 1932. His tomb was inscribed with the words:

His mind illumined the past
And the future
And wrought greatly
For the present[50]

Also on the tomb in ancient Egyptian picture writings was engraved the phrase, "I am yesterday and I know tomorrow."

During prohibition the "CPR" cave harboured a still, parts of which are still in the cavern. The cave was known as the "CPR" because of an old Canadian Pacific Railway lantern that was used to light its interior. Few know where the entranceway to this cave is. Along with the lantern and parts of the still, there is a small stove well hidden in the musty interior.

In the early 1900's spelunkers from the United States explored this part of the Grand River valley seeking evidence of caves. They were disappointed that they had such a short time to look, as they found promising evidence that caverns did exist. Despite this enticement, they never returned to continue their search. Grandmother thought they were from Kentucky where there are some famous cave systems.

In the late 1800's and early 1900's geologists drilled for oil deposits. Several natural gas wells were opened around Fergus in the 1950's. Artesian wells flow from the hills on both sides of the river, much to the consternation of residents who never know where another spring will bubble forth in a roadbed or garden. All in all, potential natural gas and oil deposits as well as ample water sources hint at potential possibly yet untapped resources.

Vinegar Hill was the southern boundary for the village. Still considered "country" in the 1940's, the summit was cropped during the summer and cattle would graze its steep slope. During the winter, the hill was the favourite ski and toboggan hill for all the young people in the area. Those with an archaeological interest knew of the site of a large Neutral Indian village in a field not far away. Occasionally artifacts were turned up by a plow, but for the most part the site remains undisturbed, even today.

A piper lived on the north bank of the river and often stood on an outcrop of limestone in the "Tangled Garden", playing his poignant music. The sound of a lone piper can send shivers up and down my spine, and I was born only one-quarter Scot. Even Grandmother, who could not be more Italian, liked the pipes. They reminded her of the Shepherd's pipes played in the hills of Northern Italy where she came from.

In the village of Gurro, Italy, not far from Vergiate where my grandmother was born, there is a legend that red-haired, blue-eyed, wild men came down from the hills to raid the village for women. Research in the 1970's proved the legend had some truth to it. The people in Gurro celebrate Robbie Burns birthday! Apparently Celts returning from southern campaigns, with the enemy in hot pursuit, hid in the mountains of Italy and Switzerland and, liking the hospitality, stayed. Some northern Italians have Celtic colouring. My father was one who was blond of hair and blue of eye.

Whistles had the power to move me from my rock and gave wings to my feet. One ate by the whistle; worked by the whistle; answered fire calls by the whistle. If children were not home from school or play at the sound of the Beatty whistle, they knew they were in trouble. Generations of Fergusites were raised to "Beatty whistle time". Even after Dad retired from Beatty Bros. he automatically rose from the dinner table at the sound of the whistle...any whistle. Dinner was promptly at 12:10. Supper was on the table at 5:30 p.m. and pity the child that dawdled. Despite the whistle, our house ran on its own time. Dad kept all our clocks fifteen minutes fast so that we would arrive, if not fifteen minutes early, at least on time. This proved an effective method of having visitors leave early. In later years it also confused a number of boyfriends who had to adjust to "Jimmy Mattaini time".

I abandoned my granite rock, not because I wanted to, but because one day I found the fence down and a bulldozer at work rearranging the hill. Developers had struck! For me, it was a sad day indeed. After a great deal of searching, and the fact that an interesting young man lived on the north side of the river, I chose the "kissing stane" in James Square as my new perch. The name for this rock came from the village legend that a boy was allowed to kiss his girl if she was sitting on the "kissing stane". In Victorian times, this was quite a liberal "legend".

Below James Square, Tower Street dips to the river gorge, crosses a bridge and continues uphill past the tennis courts, cenotaph and my family home. I can close my eyes and imagine the scene as it might have been when the area below James Square was the core of the settlement. I can smell bread and scones baking in the community bake oven. I can see Baker James Walker tending his ovens. I can smell barley roasting at the distillery. I can hear horses, oxen, teamsters; the soft swish of women's skirts, the laughter of children.

Some say I have a vivid imagination, but I hear (and sometimes feel) the past. It is the gift of parents and a grandmother who encouraged me to listen to my thoughts and to be sympathetic to history. When Grandmother would tell a story she would caution me, "Listen to me; you'll need to remember what I say many years from now". Mother has spent hours telling me what she can remember of her life and that of people around her.

One evening as I sat on the "stane", a beautiful doe picked her way through the Square. She walked down the middle of Tower Street and crossed the bridge. She turned into Queen Street heading for the quarry. Although this incident happened around 11:00 p.m., no car came along St. Andrew or Tower Street to disturb her. Perhaps she was a mirage or had I stepped back in time and she didn't belong in the present at all? I wondered about my little doe until I spoke with an old gentleman who shared my love for Fergus and the "stane". He assured me that the doe passed through often. She came from the Beaver Meadow. She has not been seen since the spring of 1989 when the beaver meadow was devoured by heavy equipment for a housing development. Like the

Templin Rock Garden.

meadow, the doe has become part of Fergus lore. Like the doe, the old gentleman too is gone, he appropriately being the last person to see her.

Much of our visual history has mercifully escaped destruction. Over two hundred and fifty buildings stand that are one hundred or more years old. Seventy-five percent of the buildings that are a century old are made of locally quarried limestone. Because the town had so little development in the 1950-60's it has retained its historic areas almost intact. Of course, there were serious fires in the business area which destroyed significant structures, but for the most part the streetscape is "Ontario Scots". Many of the older buildings have historic plaques. A walk around the tree-lined streets is a pleasant afternoon's entertainment.

One house in particular does not have a plaque. It stands on St. Andrew Street East and was the home of the "Scarlet Lady". The present owner, a spinster, decided a plaque stating occupation of owner was not exactly appropriate at this time.

If one stands on the St. David Street bridge and looks west – down the river – they will see a dam which drops the water into Mirror Basin. Look upriver and see another dam which was built across Little Falls, a substantial cascade of water. The river drops a total of forty-four feet to the Mirror Basin. The steps at Templin Gardens, a restored English Garden will lead you down to Mirror Basin. Beware of the whirlpool. It claimed

Child in Templin Garden.

its first victim in 1834 and its last in the 1970's. J.C. Templin, a man whose family was of Prussian origin, began the Templin Gardens in the 1920's. Although a teacher by vocation he could not resist the temptation to purchase the *Fergus News Record* in 1902. J.C. Templin, and his son Hugh, who was considered one of the best writers on a Canadian Weekly Press, never backed away from a controversial issue. Their newspaper became one of the best in Ontario.

If you do take the steps down to the river at Templin Gardens, be brave and walk up river from the foot of the steps to the old mill race. Stand by the ruins of the mill and you are standing at the very heart of the old settlement. With only the river's whispers to distract you, it is easy to pretend you have left the twentieth century for just a little while.

Although Fergus celebrates its Scottish heritage every August with its Scottish Festival and Highland Games, the community is equally proud of its other ethnic groups. Italians arrived in the 1880's and added their distinctive touches to the architectural styles in the area. The bowstring concrete-arched bridges through Wellington and Waterloo Counties are a tribute to Fergus' Italians – "Charlie's" bridges are a landmark fast disappearing! In the early 1900's, a number of German families moved from the Kitchener area to Fergus. With the arrival of a large number of people from Holland after the Second World War, homes and farms bloomed

Charlie Mattaini's arched bridges have played an important role throughout Wellington County. (Edith Mattaini Collection)

with prosperity as these fine people turned their talents to improving the land. Under the direction of expert cheese and butter makers, Fergus dairy products gained recognition across Canada. The cheeses were famous. Unfortunately cheese and butter are no longer made in the community as both industries were bought out by large concerns and ultimately closed down.

The arrival of our Dutch residents was akin to the influx of Irish settlers in 1851; silent acceptance, grudging admittance to their special abilities and finally, after a suitable time had elapsed, complete acceptance. In a Scots community that process could take anywhere from one to twenty-five years! Twenty years after my husband came from Africa, he was still being called "that fellow from Africa". He thought Fergus very friendly (but somewhat out of the way) because of all the people at the train station the day his family arrived. I hated to tell him that they were there to see "the black family from Africa" arrive. In reality the "German family from Africa" stepped off the train, and many people went away disappointed because "the black family" did not show!

Acceptance into the community is illustrated by the diary account written by an Irishman in 1873:

"I believe I have finally been accepted at the mill. I was called by my christian name today, and not as 'the Irishman' as is the usual fashion. I have been 'the Irishman' for three years."[51]

Scotsmen don't rush into a relationship or friendship, you know. James Straight, a brickmaker once told his wife –

"We'll give the man one year, Mary. If he don't smile, we won't hire him back. If he do, we'll pay him." [52]

Fergus, the jewel on the Grand, has a smile for everyone.

Monkland Mills, later known as Walkley's Mill. (Ted Mestern)

Present-day Fergus as captured by photographer Vern McGrath...

Walkey's Mill and mill pond, Grand River.

Along the Grand River: Templin Gardens (lower right) and Melville United Church (upper left).

The northwest corner of St. Andrew and St. David Streets.

The Post Office, with St. Andrews Church in the background.

Some Firsts for Little Falls/Fergus

First house	Begun December 20th, 1833
First contractor	Mr. Scott 1833 (Pierpoint Settlement)
First crop	Wheat, grown by William Buist
	Potatoes grown by William Buist
	Oats, grown by William Buist (1834)
First cow	Thomas Valentine
First lot sold	to William Buist, 1834
First Housekeeper	Ann Inglis, served James Webster 1834
First known settlers	Scott perhaps for a short time 1833, James Webster, James Perry, Alex D. Ferrier, Alexander Dingwall Fordyce, Charles Allan, David Blair Fergusson (all the settlement by May of 1834)
First St. Andrews Day Dinner	November 1834
First Tavern	Hugh Black, 1834
First Bridge	On Tower Street 1834
First Club	Curling Club, December 1834
First Church	St. Andrews Presbyterian, December 1834
First Baby	Adam Fergus Allan 1834
First Artist	A.D. Fordyce, 1835
First School Teacher	James MacQueen, 1835
First Millers	John Gartshore and —— Mitchell, 1835
First Druggist	James Walker (baker by trade)
First Baker	James Walker 1835
First Store	Thomas Young, 1835

First School	June 1835
First Mill	A Grist Mill, 1835
First Doctor	P.B. Henderson, 1835
First Fire	July 1835
First Postmaster	Thomas Young, 1836
First Minister	Reverend Alexander Gardiner, 1837
First Piano	Owned by Dr. William Mutch 1852
First Newspaper	*Fergus Freeholder*, 1854
First Priest	Father Demortier 1855
First Train	September 1870
First Electric Street Lights	September 14, 1884
First Phonograph	September 1891

Interior of Groves Electric Light Plant, c1892.

Endnotes

1. Letter, dated 1838 from James Webster to Reverend Patrick Bell, Webster private collection
2. Fergusson's handbook, *Practical Notes Made During a Tour in Canada and a Portion of the United States*, published 1833.
3. Letter, July 1854 from brother-in-law (Wilson) in New Zealand to Webster. Webster private collection
4. Wm. McD. Tait Collection, privately owned
5. Letter from A.D. Fordyce to Webster, Dr. A.E. Byerly collection, now in possession of author
6. The author is indebted to the National Archives of Canada, the Provincial Archives of Ontario, local land registry offices and the descendents of the Pierpoint settlement for the following information.
7. Entered page 195, Ontario Land Book A (Bundle F Misc. 1788-1795, no. 68), Archives of Ontario.
8. S.G. No. 2335 General Order in council of the 10th day of Jan. 1820, repecting Militia Grants, and Surveyor General's Ticket of Location of the 30 July 1822
9. Page 195, Ontario Land Book A (Bundle F Misc. 1788-1795, no. 68), Archives of Ontario.
10. Ibid.
11. Ibid.
12. Ibid.
13. Bell Collection, Ayrshire Scotland.
14. A Kilmarnock is a Scottish hat similar to a balmoral but a little lighter and bigger, worn flipped over at least one ear.
15. Reverend Patrick Bell Collection, privately owned, Ayrshire Scotland.
16. Original book "*The Scotsman – 1790-91*" is in the author's private collection.
17. Original book "*Heathen Customs*", 1851, published London, England; in author's private collection.
18. Archives, University of Aberdeen, Aberdeen, Scotland, AUL MS 2138.
19. National Archives, Ottawa c.1809, attributed to Absolam Shade.

20. A remittance man was a fellow that was sent away by his family (usually because of drink, but sometimes because of scandal in the family and a remittance was sent to him every month by the family to keep him out of sight in another country.

21. Published in "Hymn" (Presbyterian), Vol. 4, 1902.

22. Letter from Isabella (Barker) Lamond Smith to Clara Young, October 1989, author's private collection.

23. Dr. Abraham Groves, *All In a Day's Work*, published 1934, The Macmillan Company of Canada, Wellington County Museum and Archives.

24. Letter to Margaret (Wilson) Webster, 1876, author's private collection.

25. Letter from Granny Foote to Clara Young, September 18, 1883, in author's private collection. Letter from John Muir to John Goldie, 1936 (Goldie Collection, Guelph).

26. Dr. A.E. Byerly, *Fergus and North East Nichol*, self-published, 1933. Reprints of this book are available from the author.

27. Cathur, sometimes spelled as cawther, cauther. Cathur is a regional Lowland Scottish term for whiskey.

28. *Fergus News Record*, Christmas Edition, 1902, Wellington County Museum and Archives.

29. Wm. McD. Tait Collection.

30. *Wellington District Advocate*, Feb. 10, 1846, Reprinted in c.1933 edition *Fergus News Record*. Original newspaper located in Muir private collection.

31. Byerly Collection, in author's private collection.

32. A.D. Ferrier, *Reminiscences of Fergus*, 1865. Reprints of book are available from author.

33. From one of a series of community sketches by W.F. MacKenzie, self-styled Wellington County historian, published in area newspapers, 1903.

34. Description as appeared on Schofield map is attributed to James Webster, handwritten copy in Webster private family collection.

35. Letter from Clara Young to Aunt Elizabeth Henderson, Montreal, May 1882, in author's private collection.

36. Reverend Patrick Bell, *Journal*, 1833-36, University of Aberdeen, Aberdeen, Scotland. AUL MS #2138.

37. Letter from John Muir to John R. Goldie, 1936, Goldie Collection. Guelph.

38. Ibid.

39. Ibid.

40. Reprinted with the permission of the Henderson family.

41. Ibid.

42. Author's collection.

43. Ibid.

44. James Perry, *Reminiscences*, c.1921, reprinted in booklet form Christmas 1921.

45. Reprinted with the permission of Alexander Robertson, July 1984.

46. Reverend Patrick Bell's *Journal*, 1833-36, University of Aberdeen, Scotland,

AUL MS 2138, also National Archives, Ottawa, c.1750.

47. McDermott Collection, private.

48. Letter written by the Clerk of the Village to the Constable, 1870's, author's collection.

49. Letter written by Groves to nephew, August 1882, private Morrow Collection.

50. *The Cat's Whiskers*, Vol. 3, March 1, 1973. Official voice of Canadian Vintage Wireless Association, Fred Hammon, 81 College Avenue West, Guelph, Ontario, N1G 1S2.

51. Murphy Diaries (private Murphy Collection).

52. Taken from transcribed tape, c.1982, McDermott Collection.

Acknowledgement

Books as personal as *Fergus, A Scottish Town by Birthright,* would not be possible without the assistance of a number of people. I must thank Edith Scott Mattaini, my mother, for her invaluable support. Her well of knowledge is artesian and covers eight decades. Mother is a firm believer that for history to be enjoyed by all generations it must be treated with respect and "just a touch" of humour. Mother's sense of humour is legendary and only surpassed by her love for, and dedication to her family.

Many who should be thanked long ago passed over to what I hope is an interesting existence "on the other side". Their stories and reminiscences gave a whole new dimension to local history. Two individuals in particular, Joseph Francis Mattaini and Marie Landoni Mattaini knew how important it was to preserve verbal history and spent hours talking to me. It is unfortunate that these two individuals died before taped history was considered important. Isabel Cunningham Burr, Willard Smith, Mary Thomson and Simeon Holman must be mentioned too as being invaluable sources of information.

Thank you to the Henderson, Corcoran/Webster, Robertson, MacKenzie, Mair, Ross, Young/Barr, Murphy and McDermott families for allowing me to delve into their collections for poetry, and snippets of information to include in the book.

Wellington County Museum and Archives must be mentioned for their assistance with photographs. A special thanks to a man who died thirty-four years ago – A.E. Byerly – for being so thorough with his research; and to the late Zelma Byerly for donating some of his extensive collection to the author. Many thanks to all those individuals and families who for years have donated written and photographic materials to my personal collection and allowed unrestricted use of the same.

In closing, I must thank my husband, Ted for his support and encouragement. The hours of solitude necessary for writing are only made possible because he understands that writing is a very personal and important form of expression for me.

PAT MESTERN

Index

About the Author

Pat Mattaini Mestern was born in Fergus on July 30th, 1941. She has lived in the community all her life, a fact some people think makes her an authority on Fergus and "its happenings". Pat doesn't believe she is an authority although she does admit to knowing a great deal about  the area and its people, past and present – sometimes too much. She is the mother of four and the grandmother of three. Her first love is Ted, her husband, and her family. Her second is writing. She is the author of four previous novels: *Clara*, 1979, *Anna, Child of the Poor House*, 1981, *Rachael's Legacy*, a sequel to *Anna*, 1989 and *The Contract* (published in serial form in newspapers), 1991. Pat lives in "Clara's House" in Fergus.